JESUS
His Life and Teachings

JESUS

His Life and Teachings

As Recorded by His Friends
Matthew, Mark, Luke, and John

EDITED BY
JOSEPH F. GIRZONE

IMAGE BOOKS
DOUBLEDAY
New York   London   Toronto   Sydney   Auckland

AN IMAGE BOOK
PUBLISHED BY DOUBLEDAY
a division of Random House, Inc.
1540 Broadway, New York, New York 10036

IMAGE, DOUBLEDAY, and the portrayal of a deer
drinking from a stream are trademarks of Doubleday,
a division of Random House, Inc.

Library of Congress Cataloging-in-Publication Data
Girzone, Joseph F.
Jesus, his life and teachings: as recorded by his friends
Matthew, Mark, Luke, and John / Joseph F. Girzone.—1st Image
Book ed.
p.   cm.
1. Jesus Christ—Biography.   I. Title.
BT301.2.G53 2000
232.9′01—dc21
[B]   99-047282
CIP

5   7   9   10   8   6   4

JESUS

His Life and Teachings

ONE

This is the story of Jesus, the Anointed of God. He was also called the Son of David, an official title reserved by his people for the savior they were expecting. Jesus' lineage is traced to the father of the Hebrew people, whose name was Abraham. Some of these ancestors were good people; some were not very admirable.

This is how his life began. His mother, Mary, a virgin, was engaged to a man named Joseph, an honorable man and a skilled woodworker by trade. The couple lived in Nazareth, a town in Galilee, the northern part of Palestine, in our time the State of Israel. During their engagement but before they married, an angel appeared one day to Mary and shocked her with a strange greeting. "Hail, highly favored of God, the Lord is with you."

The young girl was frightened by the appearance of the stranger and his unusual greeting. Seeing she was confused, the angel said to her, "Do not be afraid, Mary, you have found favor with God. Behold, you will conceive and bear a son, and you shall name him Jesus. He will be great and will be called Son of the Most High, and the Lord will give him the throne of David, his father. He will rule over the house of David forever. His kingdom will last forever."

Still confused, Mary said to the angel, "How can this be since I have had no relations with a man?"

The angel replied, "The Holy Spirit will come upon you and the power of the Most High will overshadow you. The child to be born will be holy, the Son of God. To put your mind at rest, I will tell you a secret. Your cousin Elizabeth has also conceived a son in her old age, and she who was thought to be forever childless is already in her sixth month, for nothing is impossible with God."

Feeling assured, Mary said to the angel, "I am the handmaiden of the Lord. Let it be done to me according to your word." Then the angel departed.

Elizabeth and her husband, Zachary, lived in a small village named Ain-Karem barely five miles from the capital city, Jerusalem. Zachary, being of the tribe of Levi, was by birth a priest. Elizabeth was a descendant of Aaron, the first high priest, as well as the brother of Moses. The couple, widely respected for their holiness, was quite advanced in age and had long given up hope of having a child. One day, while Zachary was taking his turn offering incense in the temple in Jerusalem, an angel of the Lord appeared to him, standing at the right hand of the altar of incense. The old man became frightened and did not understand what was happening.

"Do not be afraid, Zachary," the angel said to reassure him. "Your prayer has been answered. Your wife, Elizabeth, will bear you a son, and you shall name him John. He will be the cause of much joy and will be great in the sight of the Lord. He will drink neither wine nor strong drink and will be filled with the Holy Spirit even from his mother's womb. He will turn the hearts of many in Israel to the Lord their God. He will go before him in the spirit of Elijah the prophet and cause many to ponder their lives and change their ways, to prepare a people for the Lord."

Zachary questioned the angel, "How shall I know this, for I am an old man, and my wife is advanced in years?"

The angel replied, "I am Gabriel, who stands before God. I was sent to speak to you, to announce to you the good news. But, because you have not believed my words, you will be speechless, unable to speak until all these things take place."

In the meantime, the people waiting outside were concerned because Zachary had taken so long to perform his service. When he finally appeared and they saw that he was unable to speak, they realized that he had seen a vision. He kept gesturing but could not speak. When he finished his temple duties some days later, he went back to his home.

As the angel had promised, Elizabeth did conceive. She went into seclusion for five months, thanking God for his mercy toward her. "The Lord has finally blessed me and taken away my disgrace before others."

Not long after the angel Gabriel had appeared to Mary, she left home to visit her cousin Elizabeth. It was a trip of close to one hundred miles from Nazareth to Ain-Karem. When she arrived there and entered the house, she greeted Elizabeth. When Elizabeth heard Mary's greeting, the infant leapt in her womb, and Elizabeth, filled with the Holy Spirit, burst into a song of praise. "Blessed are you among women, and truly blessed is the child in your womb. How is it that the mother of my Lord should come to visit me? For as soon as your greeting reached my ears, the child in my womb leapt for joy. Blessed are you for believing that what was prophesied to you would be fulfilled."

Then Mary burst into poetic song. "My soul proclaims the greatness of the Lord, and my spirit rejoices in God my savior. He has looked upon the lowliness of his handmaid.

From now on, all ages will call me blessed, for he who is mighty has done great things for me, and holy is his name. From generation to generation is his mercy to those who revere him. He has shown his great strength, scattering the wicked in their pride. He has dethroned the mighty and exalted the lowly. The rich he has dispossessed. He has strengthened his servant Israel, ever mindful of his past mercy, as he had promised to our father Abraham and to his descendants forever."

Mary stayed with her cousin for three months, then returned to her own home.

Shortly afterward, Elizabeth gave birth to her son. All her friends and family came to visit her and pay their respects. Eight days later, as was the custom, the family gathered for the baby's circumcision. Everyone expected he would be named after his father, Zachary. Elizabeth told them, however, his name would be John. "Why? There is no one by that name in the family," the family protested. Beckoning for Zachary's attention, they asked him what name he wanted to give the baby. On a writing tablet he wrote, "His name is John." Everyone was shocked. At that moment, Zachary's voice returned and he began to speak, thanking God for all the wonderful things that had happened.

The guests stood in awe of what they were witnessing and could not wait to tell all their neighbors. They knew God had destined this child for something special, so they kept all that happened in their hearts to see what would later become of the child.

Overcome with emotion and inspired by the Holy Spirit, Zachary burst into prophetic song:

"Blessed be the Lord, the God of Israel, because he has visited and brought redemption to his people. He has given us a mighty savior from the house of David his servant. This he had always promised through the lips of the prophets even from ancient times: salvation from our enemies and from the grip of those who hate us. Showing mercy to our forebears, ever mindful of his holy covenant, which he swore in oath to our father Abraham, that freed from our enemies, we would serve him without fear, in integrity and holiness of life all our days. And you, child, will be called the prophet of the Most High, because it is you who will go before the Lord to prepare his way, opening the minds and hearts of his people, announcing to them his coming, and preaching to them forgiveness of their sins, reminding them of the kindness of God who has sent the sun from on high to visit us, and to shine on those who sit in darkness and in fear of death, and to guide us into a new life of peace."

As the child grew in age, he also grew stronger in body and spirit. As a young boy, he left home and lived in the wilderness, growing ever closer to God, until the day when the Lord called him to begin his mission.

TWO

Not long after Mary returned home, it came
to the attention of Joseph, to whom she was engaged, that
she was pregnant. He was deeply offended, since he loved
and trusted her. He felt that, in justice, he could not continue their relationship, but not wishing to disgrace her
publicly, he decided to divorce her privately. (Engagement
in those days was equivalent to marriage, and to break an
engagement with someone was the same as divorcing the
person.)

Having a difficult time arriving at a decision, he prayed
and asked God for guidance. One night, in a dream, an
angel of the Lord appeared to him and told him, "Joseph,

do not be afraid to take Mary as your wife, for the child in her womb is of the Holy Spirit. She will have a son, and you are to name him Jesus, because he will save his people from their sins."

This took place in fulfillment of the prophecy of Isaiah, who prophesied: "Behold, the virgin shall conceive and bear a son. They shall call him Emmanuel (which means 'God with us')."

Following the instructions of the angel, Joseph went ahead with his plans to marry Mary.

Eventually, the time came for Mary's delivery. It coincided with a decree issued by Caesar Augustus, ordering a census throughout the Roman Empire. It was during the reign of Cyrinus, governor of the province of Syria. Each person was required to register at the town of their family's origins. Being of the house of David, both Joseph and Mary had to register in a small village called Bethlehem, some ninety miles south, in Judea, which was where their ancestor King David was born and raised.

Finding a fitting place for the child to be born was futile, as it seemed no one would welcome Joseph and his pregnant wife. They finally found an animal shelter outside the village, and Mary gave birth to her child, wrapped him in swaddling bands, and placed him in a feeding trough, which is sometimes called a manger.

Meanwhile, shepherds living in the nearby fields and watching over their sheep that night saw a bright light in the sky, which they recognized as an angel of the Lord. They became frightened. But the angel said to them, "Do not be afraid, for, behold, I bring you joyful tidings, news of great joy for the whole world. There has been born to you today in the town of David, a savior, who is Christ the Lord. If you need a sign, you will find an infant wrapped in banding and lying in a feedbox." Immediately, the heavens were filled with a choir of angels singing, "Glory to God in the highest heaven, and peace on earth to people of goodwill."

When the angels left, the shepherds, convinced that what they had experienced was a message from God, left immediately and found Mary and Joseph and the child lying in the manger as the angel had told them. They were deeply moved by what they had seen and began to understand something of the mystery the angels had shared with them. They told Mary and Joseph about the vision they had seen in the fields and the message the angel had given to them. Mary was overwhelmed with all that was happening and kept turning over in her mind all the things that were taking place. When the shepherds left, they could not wait to tell the whole neighborhood what they had seen. The people were thrilled with the news. They had been expecting the savior promised by God to come at any time. The shepherds returned to their flocks, filled with joy, praising God for the wonderful things they had experienced.

What had happened was truly a mystery, the mystery of God taking on the form of a human being. Before time began, this child came from the mind of God, sharing God's own being. He was truly the Word, the very reflection of God proceeding from the mind of God, and now coming into this world, the Word made flesh, dwelling among us, revealing his glory as the only begotten of the Father, full of holiness and goodness.

Before time began, the Word existed with God. Indeed, the Word was God, and all things came into being through him. In him was life itself. This life now became the light for all humankind, for all, that is, who chose to follow the light. That light shone in the darkness, but the darkness refused to accept it, because it preferred the darkness to the light.

Eight days after the birth of the child, his parents presented him for circumcision. This was a sacred rite for the Jewish people, as it was the sign of the covenant between God and the people he had chosen for a special destiny. At that ceremony the child was given the name Jesus, the name given him by the angel before he had been conceived in his mother's womb.

On the fortieth day after the birth of the child, when his mother's period of ritual purification ended, his parents brought him to the temple at Jerusalem and presented him to God, as a male child in those days was considered especially holy. Joseph and Mary offered the sacrifice prescribed for the poor: "a pair of turtle doves or two young pigeons."

There was at the time a holy man living in Jerusalem whose name was Simeon. He spent much time in the temple, praying. Because of Simeon's holiness, God promised to grant him his lifelong wish to live long enough to see the Messiah, the savior of his people. Inspired by the Holy Spirit, he had gone up to the temple that day to pray. Seeing Mary and Joseph as they were presenting the child Jesus to the Lord, he knew his prayer had been answered. Walking over to them, he took the child in his arms and praised God with the words:

> "Now, Lord, you may dismiss your servant in peace according to your word, for my eyes have seen your salvation, which you have prepared in the sight of all peoples, a light of revelation to the Gentiles and the glory of your people Israel."

The child's parents were amazed at the words of the holy man, who then blessed them and said to the mother, "Behold, this child is destined for the rise and the fall of many in Israel, and a sign that will be contradicted. Your own soul a sword will pierce that the thoughts of many will be revealed."

In the temple at the same time was an elderly prophetess, a widow named Anna, the daughter of Phanuel of the tribe of Aser. She was of great age, having lived with her husband for many years, then as a widow until she was eighty-four. In fact, she never left the temple, but worshiped night and day, praying and fasting. Arriving at that very time, she witnessed what was happening. Immediately, she broke out in prophecy and thanked God for the coming of the child. Wandering about the temple precincts, she spoke about the child to all who were awaiting the redemption of Jerusalem.

When the parents had fulfilled all the prescriptions of the law, they returned home to Nazareth, their village in Galilee. The child grew, not only in age but also in wisdom and grace before God. (Shortly afterward, however, the family returned to Bethlehem, where they took up residence.)

As time passed, magi, or wise men, came from the east into Judea in search of the newborn king. Not knowing where to find him, they asked the people in Jerusalem where he had been born. "We have seen his star at its rising and have come with gifts to do him homage." When Herod, the king of Judea, heard this, he was greatly disturbed, as was all Jerusalem with him. Assembling all the chief priests and the scribes, experts in the law, he inquired of them where the Messiah was to be born. They told him, "In Bethlehem of Judea, for thus it has been written through the prophet: 'And you, Bethlehem, land of Judah, are by no means least among the rulers of Judah, for from you shall come a ruler, who is to shepherd my people Israel.' "

Then Herod summoned the magi secretly and ascertained from them the time of the star's appearance. He sent them to Bethlehem and said, "Go and search diligently for the child. When you have found him, bring me word that I, too, may go and pay him homage." After their audience with the king, they set out. And to their surprise, the star that they had seen at its rising preceded them, until it came and stopped over the place where the child was. They were filled with joy at seeing the star, and on entering the house they saw the child with Mary, his mother, and, falling to their knees, they did him homage. Then they opened their presents and offered him gifts of gold, frankincense, and myrrh.

Having been warned in a dream not to return to Herod, they went back to their country by another route.

After the magi departed, an angel of the Lord appeared to Joseph in a dream, telling him: "Take the child and his mother, flee to Egypt, and stay there until I tell you. Herod is going to search for the child to destroy him." Joseph rose and took the child and his mother by night and left for Egypt. He stayed there until the death of Herod, that the words spoken through the prophet Hosea might be fulfilled: "Out of Egypt I have called my son."

When Herod realized he had been deceived by the magi, he became enraged and immediately ordered the massacre of all the boys in Bethlehem and the surrounding area two years old and younger, calculating from the time of the star's first appearance to the magi. Thus was fulfilled the prophecy spoken by Jeremiah: "A voice was heard in Ramah, sobbing and loud lamentation; Rachel weeping for her children, and she would not be consoled, because they were no more."

Not long afterward, Herod died and was succeeded by his son Archelaus. The angel again appeared in a dream to Joseph in Egypt, and told him, "Arise, take the child and his mother and return to the land of Israel. Those who sought the life of the child are dead." Joseph arose, took the child and his mother, and returned to the land of Israel. But when he heard that Archelaus was ruling over Judea in place of his father, he was afraid to go back there. Having been warned in a dream, he returned to Nazareth instead, which is in Galilee, that the prophecies might be fulfilled, which said, "He shall be called a Nazorean."

As was their custom, the parents of Jesus went to Jerusalem each year to celebrate the feast of Passover, the sacred time during which Jews commemorate the avenging angel's passing over Egypt, where their ancient ancestors were enslaved. (It was on that occasion that their people were set free from slavery by God's intervention.) The boy Jesus had now reached his twelfth birthday and, being considered a man in his religion, would commit himself to its law. As a son of the law, he was entitled to all its privileges as well as its responsibilities. When the ceremony ended, the parents started on their way home, but on the way, when the men and women met at camp outside the city (as they had to worship separately in the temple), Joseph and Mary realized that the boy was with neither of them. They searched for him among their relatives and acquaintances in the camp. Not finding him, they rushed back to the city. After three days they found him in the temple, sitting in the midst of the teachers, listening to them and asking them questions. All who heard him were astonished at his understanding and the wisdom of his answers.

When his parents found him, they were in shock. His mother said to him, "Son, why have you done this to us? Your father and I have been looking for you with great anxiety."

His response was "Why were you looking for me? Did you not know that I must be about my Father's business?" But they did not understand what he said to them.

However, he went down with them to Nazareth and remained obedient to them, advancing in wisdom and age and grace before God and man. His mother, meanwhile, kept all these things in her heart.

THREE

*M**any years later*, in the fifteenth year of the reign of Tiberius Caesar, when Pontius Pilate was governor of Judea, and Herod Antipas was tetrarch of Galilee, and his brother Philip, tetrarch of the region of Ituraea and Trachonitis, and Lysanias was tetrarch of Abilene, and while Annas and Caiaphas were high priests, the word of God came to John in the desert. John, remember, was Jesus' cousin, the child of Elizabeth and Zachary, the priest. John went about the whole region of the Jordan River, proclaiming a baptism of repentance for the forgiveness of sins, as is written in the book of the words of the prophet Isaiah: "A voice of one crying in the desert: 'Prepare the way of the

Lord, make straight his paths. Every valley shall be filled and every mountain and hill shall be made low. The winding roads shall be made straight, and the rough ways smooth, and all flesh shall see the salvation of God.' "

John preached a strong message to the people who came out to be baptized by him. "You brood of vipers! Who warned you to flee from the wrath to come? Produce good fruits as evidence of your repentance, and do not say to yourselves 'We have Abraham for our father,' for I tell you, God can raise up children to Abraham from these very stones. Even now the ax is laid to the root of the trees. Every tree that does not bear good fruit will be cut down and thrown into the fire."

The crowds asked him, "What is it that we should do?" He told them, "Whoever has two cloaks should share with him who has none. Whoever has food should do likewise." Even tax collectors came to be baptized. They asked him what was expected of them. He told them, "Stop collecting more than what is prescribed." Soldiers also asked him, "And what is it that we should do?" He told them, "Do not extort money from people, do not falsely accuse anyone, and be content with your pay."

The power of John's message filled the people with expectation, and they wondered if he might be the Messiah, the savior that was to come. "Who are you?" they asked him. "I am not the Messiah." "Who, then?" they continued asking him. "Are you Elijah, the prophet who is to return?"

"I am not." "Are you the prophet?" "No," he replied. "Who are you, then, so we can give some answer to those who sent us? What do you have to say for yourself?"

"I am the voice of one crying in the wilderness, 'Make straight the way of the Lord,' as Isaiah the prophet said."

Some Pharisees, who belonged to the strictest sect in the Jewish religion, were also sent, and they asked him, "Why do you baptize if you are not the Messiah, or Elijah, or the prophet?" "I baptize with water, but one mightier than I is coming, who will baptize you with the Holy Spirit and fire. I am not even worthy to untie the straps of his sandals. His winnowing fan is already in his hand to clear the threshing floor and to gather the wheat into his barn, but the chaff he will burn with unquenchable fire."

Exhorting them in many other ways, he preached good news to the people. In the meantime, Herod, the tetrarch, who had been censured by John because he married Herodias, his brother's wife, and because of other evil things he did, eventually put John into prison, but not before John met and baptized Jesus.

This meeting took place one day while John was baptizing. Jesus came up and approached him. As John saw him approaching, moved by the Spirit of God, he cried out, "Behold the Lamb of God, who takes away the sins of the world. He is the one of whom I said, 'A man is coming after me who ranks ahead of me because he existed before me.' I did not know him, but the reason why I came baptizing with water was that he might be made known to Israel." Jesus asked John to baptize him. John was reluctant. "It is I who should be baptized by you, yet you come to me and ask to be baptized." Jesus told him, "Let it be so for now, for it is fitting that I should fulfill what others must fulfill in following God's will." Then John baptized him.

After Jesus walked up from the water, and was praying, the Spirit of God descended upon him in the form of a dove, and a voice came out of the heavens, saying, "This is my beloved Son, in whom I am well pleased."

John later testified to this, saying, "I saw the Spirit come down like a dove from the sky and remain upon him. I did not know him, but the one who sent me to baptize with water told me, 'On whomever you see the Spirit come down and remain, he is the one who will baptize with the Holy Spirit.' Now I have seen and testified that he is the Son of God."

This took place in Bethany, across the Jordan, where John was baptizing.

The next day Jesus was led by the Spirit into the desert to be tempted by the devil. He fasted for forty days and forty nights, and afterward was hungry. The devil approached and said to him, "If you are the Son of God, command these stones become loaves of bread." Jesus said in reply, "It is written, 'Not on bread alone does one live, but on every word that comes from the mouth of God.' "

Then the devil took him to the holy city, and, standing him on the parapet of the temple, said to him, "If you are the Son of God, cast yourself down, for it is written, 'He will command his angels concerning you' and 'with their hands they will support you, lest you dash your foot against a stone.' "

Jesus answered him, "It is also written, 'You shall not put the Lord, your God, to the test.' "

Then the devil took him up to a very high mountain, and, showing him all the kingdoms of the earth in their magnificence, said to him, "All these I shall give you if you will fall down and worship me."

At that, Jesus said to him, "Begone, Satan! It is written, 'The Lord, your God, shall you worship, and Him alone shall you serve.' "

Then the devil left him and angels came and ministered to him.

Leaving the wilderness, Jesus wandered the Jordan River, where John was preaching and baptizing. With John in those days were two of his disciples. Noticing Jesus walking past, he spoke out: "Behold, the Lamb of God!" Hearing this, the two disciples followed Jesus. Noticing them following him, Jesus turned and asked them, "What are you looking for?" They said to him, "Rabbi, [meaning "teacher" in Hebrew], where are you staying?" "Come and see," he responded to them. So they went and saw where he was staying, and they stayed with him that day. It was about four in the afternoon.

Andrew, the brother of Simon Peter, was one of the two

who heard John and followed Jesus. He then went and found his brother Simon and said to him, "We have found the Messiah." Then he brought him to Jesus. Jesus looked at him and said, "You are Simon, the son of John; you will be called Kephas" (which is translated "Rock").

After this, Jesus and his disciples went into the outlying area of Judea and spent some time there with them baptizing. John was also baptizing in Aenon near Salim, because there was an abundance of water there, and people came to be baptized, for John had not as yet been imprisoned.

Now a dispute arose between the disciples of John and a certain Jew about ceremonial washings. So they came to John and said to him, "Teacher, the one who was with you across the Jordan, about whom you testified, he is baptizing and everyone is coming to him."

John answered and said, "No one can claim anything as his own unless it is given him from heaven. You yourselves are witnesses to what I told you, 'I myself am not the Christ; I am the one sent to precede him. The bride is for the bridegroom only. Yet the bridegroom's friend, who stands there and listens, is glad when he hears the bridegroom's voice.' This same joy I feel and now my joy is complete. He must grow in stature, while I am content to fade away. He who comes from above is above all others; he who is born of the earth is earthly himself, and speaks in an earthly way. He who comes from heaven bears witness to the things he has seen and heard even if there are those who refuse to believe.

21

Those who accept his testimony, however, bear witness to the truthfulness of God, since he whom God has sent speaks the words of God, as God gives him his Spirit freely and in full measure. The Father loves the Son, and has entrusted everything to him, and anyone who believes in the Son has eternal life. Anyone who refuses to accept the Son will never see eternal life, for the displeasure of God rests on him."

Arriving in Galilee, he found Philip. Jesus said to him, "Follow me!" Philip was from Bethsaida, the town of Andrew and Peter. Philip found Nathaniel and told him, "We have found the one whom Moses wrote about in the law, and also the prophets, Jesus, the son of Joseph, from Nazareth."

Nathaniel said to him, "Can any good come out of Nazareth?" Philip said, "Come and see."

When Jesus saw Nathaniel coming toward him, he said of him, "Behold a true Israelite in whom there is no deceit." Nathaniel responded, "How do you know me?" To which Jesus replied, "Before Philip called you, I saw you under the fig tree."

Nathaniel answered him, "Rabbi, you are the Son of God; you are the King of Israel."

Jesus said to him, "Do you believe because I told you I saw you under the fig tree? Greater things than this you will witness. You will one day see the sky opened and the angels of God ascending and descending on the Son of Man."

Wandering from village to village in Galilee, Jesus preached in the synagogues and was praised by all.

Stopping in Nazareth, where he grew up, his reputation had preceded him. As was his custom, he entered the synagogue on the sabbath, and got up to read. He was given the scroll of the prophet Isaiah. He unrolled the scroll and found the passage where it was written:

"The Spirit of the Lord is upon me,
   because he has anointed me
   to bring good news to the poor.
He has sent me to bring liberty to captives
   and recovery of sight to the blind;
   to free those in bondage,
   and proclaim a year acceptable to the Lord."

Rolling up the scroll, he handed it back to the attendant and sat down. The eyes of all in the synagogue were upon him. He said to them, "Today, this scripture passage is fulfilled in your hearing." All spoke highly of him and were amazed at the gracious words that flowed from his lips. Where did he get all this wisdom, and this power to work such wonders? They also asked, "Is not this the carpenter, the son of Joseph and Mary, the mother of James and Joses and Simon and Jude. And his sisters, are they not also with us?" And they found it hard to accept him.

He said to them, "Surely, you will quote me the proverb, 'Physician, cure yourself,' and say, 'Do here in your hometown the things we heard were done in Capernaum.' " And he said to them, "In truth, I tell you, no prophet is accepted in his own country, or among his own relatives, or even in his own house. Indeed, I tell you, there were many widows in Israel in the days of Elijah the prophet, when the sky was closed for three and a half years, and a severe famine spread across the entire land. But it was to none of them was Elijah sent, only to a widow in Zarephath in the land of Sidon. Again, there were many lepers in Israel in the time of Elisha, yet not one of them was cleansed, but only Naaman, the Syrian."

When the people in the synagogue heard this, they were filled with anger. Rising up, they drove him out of the town to the brow of the hill, where they intended to hurl him down headlong, but he passed through their midst and went away. Jesus was shocked that they found it so difficult to believe in him. As a result, he could work no miracles there, except for curing a few sick people by laying his hands on them.

FOUR

After leaving Nazareth, he went down to Capernaum near the sea and settled there, in the region of Zebulun and Naphtali, thus fulfilling the prophecy:

"Land of Zebulun, and land of Naphtali, the way by the sea,
    beyond the Jordan, Galilee of the nations,
    the people who live in darkness have seen a great light.
    On those dwelling in the shadowed land of death, a light has risen."

It was at that time that Jesus began preaching the message "Repent, the kingdom of God is near at hand." One day as he was walking along the seashore, a large crowd gathered around him to hear the word of God. As the pressure of the crowd threatened, he came across two brothers, Simon, called Peter (Rock), and his brother Andrew, casting a net into the sea; they were fishermen. Getting into one of the boats, the one belonging to Simon, he told him to push away from the land. Then he sat down and taught the large crowd from the boat. After he had finished speaking, he told Simon, "Go out into deeper water and lower your nets for a catch." "Master," Peter protested, "we have been working hard at it all night and have caught nothing, but if you tell me, I will lower the nets."

As soon as they had done this, they caught a huge number of fish, so many, the nets were beginning to tear. They signaled to their partners in the other boat to come and help them. They came and filled both boats to the point where they were in danger of sinking. Seeing this, Simon Peter fell down on his knees before Jesus, saying, "Depart from me, Lord, for I am a sinful man." Astonishment at the huge catch of fish struck him and all those with him, and likewise James and John, Zebedee's sons, who were partners of Simon.

"Do not be afraid," he said to them, "from now on, you will follow me, and I will make you fishers of men." Arriving at shore, they left everything at once and followed him.

At that time, there was a wedding in Cana in Galilee. The mother of Jesus was invited, as well as her son and his disciples. On the third day, Jesus arrived with his disciples. When the wine ran short, Jesus' mother said to him, "Son, they have no wine."

Jesus replied, "Woman, how does that concern us? My appointed time has not yet come."

His mother went to the waiters and instructed them, "Do whatever he tells you."

There were six stone water jars for Jewish ceremonial washings, each containing between twenty to thirty gallons. Jesus told them, "Fill the jars with water." They filled them to the brim. Then he told them, "Now draw some out and take it to the chief steward."

They did so, and when the chief steward tasted the water which had become wine, not knowing where it came from (though the waiters who had drawn the water knew), the chief steward called the bridegroom and said to him, "Everyone serves good wine first, then, when people have drunk freely, an inferior vintage, but you have kept the best until last."

Jesus did this, the first of his signs, in Cana in Galilee, allowing his glory to be seen, and his disciples began to believe in him. After this, he and his mother and the brothers went down to Capernaum and stayed there only a few days.

He went about Galilee, teaching in the synagogues, proclaiming the good news of the kingdom and curing every disease and illness among the people. His fame spread to all of Syria, and they brought to him all who were sick with disease and other painful ailments, as well as those possessed of evil spirits, and epilepsy, and those paralyzed, and he cured them. Great crowds from Galilee, the Decapolis, Jerusalem, Judea, and from across the Jordan followed him.

While at Capernaum, he entered the synagogue on the sabbath and taught. The people were astonished at his teaching, for he taught with authority and not like the scribes. In their synagogue there was a man possessed by an unclean spirit. He cried out, "What have you to do with us, Jesus of Nazareth? Have you come to destroy us? We know who you are: the Holy One of God." Jesus ordered him, "Be quiet, and come out of the man." The unclean spirit threw the man into convulsions and, shrieking loudly, came out of him. Astonished, the people asked one another, "What does this mean? An entirely new teaching, and spoken with authority; he even gives orders to unclean spirits and they obey him." His reputation spread throughout the area, and the whole Galilean countryside.

When it was evening, after sunset, they brought to him all who were ill or possessed by evil spirits. The whole town gathered at the door (where he was speaking). He cured many who were sick with various diseases, and drove out the evil spirits, not allowing them to speak, because they knew who he was.

As he was teaching, Pharisees and those learned in the law were sitting in the crowd. They had come from every village in Galilee, Judea, and Jerusalem, and the Spirit of God was pressing on Jesus to heal. Some men had been trying to bring to Jesus a paralyzed man on a stretcher, but they could not reach him because of the crowd. Not finding a way, they went up on the roof and lifted off the tiles, letting the stretcher down through the roof to the feet of Jesus.

When he saw their faith, he said to the paralyzed man, "Your sins are forgiven." Hearing this, the scribes and Pharisees began to murmur, "Who is this who dares to speak such blasphemies? Who but God can forgive sins?"

Knowing their thoughts, Jesus said to them, "Why do you think such thoughts? Which is easier, to say 'Your sins are forgiven'? or to say 'Rise and walk'?" But to show that the Son of Man has power on earth to forgive sins, he said to the paralyzed man, "Take up your stretcher and go home!"

The man stood up, took up his stretcher, and went home, shouting praise and thanks to God. Awe seized the whole crowd as they said, "We have seen incredible happenings today."

Rising early, long before dawn, he left and went off to a deserted place to pray. Simon and those who were with him went out looking for him. Finding him, they said, "Everyone is looking for you." He responded, "Let us go to the neighboring villages that I may preach there also. For this is the reason I have come." So he traveled throughout the Galilean countryside, preaching and driving out evil spirits.

Passing through towns and villages, he came across a tax collector named Levi, sitting at his counting booth. Jesus said to him, "Follow me!" Leaving everything, he got up immediately and followed him. Shortly afterward he threw a banquet for him in his house. A large crowd of tax collectors and others were at table with them.

The Pharisees and scribes complained to his disciples, saying, "Why do you eat and drink with tax collectors and sinners?"

Jesus said to them, "Those who are healthy do not need a physician, only sick people do. I have not come to call the righteous to repentance, but sinners."

Then they said to him, "The disciples of John fast often and offer prayers, and the disciples of the Pharisees do the same, but yours enjoy eating and drinking."

Jesus answered them, "How can you tell the wedding guests to fast when the bridegroom is with them? When the day comes and the bridegroom is taken away, then they will surely fast." He also told them a parable. "No one uses a piece of new cloth to patch an old cloak, otherwise, when the cloak is washed, the new patch will shrink and tear away from the fabric, and the hole will be worse than before. Similarly, no one puts new wine into old wineskins, otherwise, when the new wine ferments, it will burst the old wineskins and all will be lost. No, you put new wine into fresh wineskins. Nobody drinking old wine would want new wine, for he says, 'The old is good.' "

While he was still speaking to them, an official came up to him, bowed down before him, and said, "My daughter has just died, but come and lay your hand on her and she will be saved."

Jesus stopped what he was doing, and, together with his disciples, followed him. Unexpectedly, a woman who had been hemorrhaging for twelve years came up behind Jesus and touched the fringe of his cloak. She was thinking, "If only I can touch his cloak, I shall be saved."

Jesus turned and saw her. He said to her, "Courage, my daughter, your faith has saved you." At that very moment, the woman was healed.

When Jesus reached the official's house and saw the flute players, and the crowd creating a scene, he said, "Leave her, the little girl is not dead. She is only sleeping." They ridiculed him.

When the people left, Jesus went inside and took the girl's hand, and she got up. The news of this spread all throughout the countryside.

As Jesus continued on his way, two blind men followed him, shouting, "Take pity on us, Son of David." When Jesus reached the house where he was going, the blind men approached him. Turning to them, he said, "Do you believe I can do this?"

They said, "Lord, we do."

Then he touched their eyes and said, "Let it be done to you according to your faith." At that their sight returned. Jesus then strictly warned them, "Tell no one of this!" But when they left, they told everyone they met throughout the neighborhood about what had happened.

In time Jesus toured all the towns and villages, teaching in their synagogues and proclaiming the good news of the kingdom, and curing all kinds of diseases and illnesses. Seeing the large crowds, he felt sorry for them because they were so anxious and depressed, like sheep without a shepherd. He said to his disciples, "The harvest is rich, but the laborers are few. Ask the Lord of the harvest to send laborers to his harvest."

One day, as Jesus and his disciples were walking through a field of standing grain on the sabbath, his disciples were picking the heads off the stalks, rubbing them in their hands, and eating them. Some Pharisees complained, "Why are you doing what is not lawful on the sabbath?"

Jesus said in reply, "Have you not read what David [King David was the beloved hero king of years past] did during the reign of Abiathar, the high priest, when he and his companions were hungry? And how he went into the house of God and took the sacred showbread [symbolizing the presence of God in the community] which only the priests were allowed to eat, and ate it, after sharing it with his companions. And have you not read in the law where it says the temple priests in performing their duties may violate the sabbath without committing sin. I tell you, there is something here greater than the temple. Had you understood the meaning of the words 'It is mercy I desire, not sacrifices,' you would not have been so quick to condemn the innocent. The sabbath was made for people, not people for the sabbath. And I tell you further, the Son of Man is Lord even of the sabbath."

On another sabbath, he entered a synagogue and began to teach. There was in the room a man with a withered hand. The Pharisees were watching to see if Jesus would heal him on the sabbath, hoping to catch him doing something they could use against him. Knowing their thoughts, he said to the man with the withered hand, "Stand up and come out here in front of everyone." The man came and stood there. Then Jesus said to the Pharisees, "Is it lawful to do good on the sabbath, or to do evil on the sabbath? To save a life or let it be destroyed? Who among you, if you had one sheep and it fell into a hole on the sabbath, would not lift it out? Now, a human being is much more precious than a sheep, so it is therefore permissible to do good on the sabbath." Looking around at them all, he then said to the man with the withered hand, "Stretch out your hand." He did so, and his hand became perfectly normal. The Pharisees were furious and began to plot against Jesus.

It was about this time that Jesus left and went into the hills to pray, spending the whole day communing with God. When the following day came, he called together his disciples, and from the group he picked twelve, whom he called apostles (meaning persons who are sent on a mission): Simon, whom he named Peter; his brother Andrew; James; John; Philip; Bartholomew; Matthew; Thomas; James, the son of Alphaeus; Simon, called the Zealot; Judas (Thaddeus), son of James; and Judas, who was to betray him.

He then went home again, and as soon as he appeared, such a huge crowd began to gather that there was not even time to eat a meal. When his relatives heard of this, they went to rescue him, for they thought he was beside himself. When his mother and his brothers arrived, they sent word to him to come with them. A crowd seated around him told him, "Your mother and your brothers are outside, asking for you."

He said to them, "Who are my mother and my brothers?" Looking around at those seated in the circle, he said, "These are my mother and my brothers. Whoever does the will of God is my brother and sister and mother."

There were scribes and Pharisees there who had come from Jerusalem. The people brought to Jesus a blind man who was also possessed by an evil spirit who made him dumb. Jesus cured him, and the man could see and began to speak. The people were amazed, and they remarked, "Could this not be the Son of David [a title for the promised savior]?" But the scribes and Pharisees were saying, "He is possessed by Beelzebul, the prince of devils, and by the prince of devils he drives out demons."

Summoning them, he began to speak to them in parables. "How can Satan drive out Satan? If a kingdom is divided against itself, it cannot stand. And if a household is divided against itself, it will fall apart. If Satan is divided against himself, then he cannot endure. That is the end of him. No one can enter a strong man's house and plunder his property unless he first disarms the strong man. In truth, anyone who is not with me is against me, and anyone who does not gather with me cause many to be lost. I tell you solemnly, sins and all blasphemies people utter will be forgiven them, but whoever blasphemes against the Holy Spirit will never be forgiven, but is guilty of a sin that will never end [because they refuse to acknowledge and accept the one who brings them God's forgiveness and life]." For they said, "He has an evil spirit."

FIVE

Sometime later, Jesus returned to Capernaum. When word got around that he was back, the crowds began to gather. He went up on the mountainside and sat down. His disciples gathered around him, and he began to teach them:

"Blessed are the poor in spirit, for theirs is the kingdom of heaven.

Blessed are they who mourn, for they will be comforted.

Blessed are the meek, for they will inherit the land.

Blessed are they who hunger and thirst for righteousness, for they will be satisfied.

Blessed are the merciful, for they shall be treated with mercy.

Blessed are the single-hearted, for they shall see God.

Blessed are the peacemakers, for they shall be called the children of God.

And blessed are they who are persecuted in the pursuit of what is right, for theirs is the kingdom of heaven.

And blessed are you when they abuse you and persecute you, and speak every evil thing against you because of me, for your reward in heaven will be great. They persecuted the prophets before you in just the same way.

"You are the salt of the earth, but if the salt loses its taste, who can restore its flavor? It is no longer good for anything, but to be thrown out and walked upon. You are the light of the world. A city set on a mountaintop cannot be hidden. Nor do they light a lamp, then put it under a bushel basket; it is set on a lamp-stand, where it shines upon everyone in the house. In the same way, your light must shine before all, so everyone can see your good works and glorify your Father in heaven.

"Do not think I have come to abolish the law and the

prophets. I have come, not to abolish, but to fulfill. In truth, I say to you, until heaven and earth pass away, not one mark or one dot of the law will be done away with until it is all fulfilled. Therefore, whoever breaks one of the least of the commandments and teaches others to do so shall be considered least in the kingdom of heaven. Whoever obeys and teaches these commandments will be considered great in the kingdom of heaven. But I warn you, unless your righteousness has more depth than that of the scribes and Pharisees, you will not even enter the kingdom of heaven.

"You have heard it was said to your ancestors, 'You shall not kill; and whoever kills will be liable to judgment.' But I say to you, whoever is angry with his brother will be liable to judgment, and whoever calls his brother 'Idiot' will be brought before the Sanhedrin. And whoever calls his brother 'Misfit' he will be liable to the fires of hell. [All these actions express profound hatred and contempt, which is offensive to God.] Therefore, if you are about to lay your gift upon the altar, then recall that your brother has something against you, leave your gift at the altar, go reconcile yourself with your brother, then come and offer your gift. Settle with your opponent quickly while on the way to court with him. Otherwise, your opponent will hand you over to the judge, who will hand you over to the guard, and you will be thrown into prison. In truth, I tell you, you will not be released until you have paid the last penny.

"You have heard it said, 'You shall not commit adultery.'

But I say to you, whoever looks at a woman with lust has already committed adultery with her in his heart. If your right eye causes you to sin, tear it out, and throw it away. It is better to lose one of your members than to have your whole body thrown into hell [the place of everlasting punishment]. And if your right hand causes you to sin, cut it off and throw it away. It is better to lose one of your members than to have your whole body go into hell.

"It was also said, 'Whoever divorces his wife must give her a bill of divorce.' But I say to you, whoever divorces his wife [unlawful union excepted] and marries another causes his wife to commit adultery, and anyone who marries a divorced woman commits adultery.

"Again, you have heard that it was said to your ancestors, 'Do not take a false oath, but make good your oaths to the Lord.' But I say to you, do not swear at all, either by heaven, since it is God's throne, nor by the earth, as it is God's footstool, nor by Jerusalem, since it is the city of the great king. Do not swear by your own head either, since you cannot turn a single hair white or black. Let your answer be 'yes' if you mean yes, or 'no' if you mean no. Anything more than that is from the evil one.

"You have heard that it was said, 'An eye for an eye, and a tooth for a tooth.' But I say to you, offer no resistance to mean people. On the contrary, if anyone slaps you on the one cheek, offer him the other. If a man takes you to law and demands your tunic, let him have your cloak as well. If anyone orders you to go one mile, go two miles with him. Give to anyone who asks, and do not refuse anyone who wants to borrow.

"You have learned that it was said, 'You shall love your neighbor, but hate your enemy.' But I say to you, love your enemies, and pray for those who persecute you, that you may be children of your Father in heaven, for he causes the sun to shine on the good as well as the bad, and his rain to fall on the just as well as on the unjust. For if you love those who love you, why should you expect reward for that? Do not even tax collectors do as much? And if you welcome your brothers only, what credit is that to you, do not even heathens do as much. In truth, be perfect the way your heavenly Father is perfect: in love.

"When you perform good deeds, do not do it publicly for show. If you do, do not expect a reward from your heavenly Father, for you already have your reward. And when you give money to the poor, do not blow a trumpet announcing your arrival, as the hypocrites in the synagogues and on the street corners for people's praise. In truth, I tell you, they already have their reward. But when you give alms, do not let your left hand know what your right hand is doing, so that your almsgiving may be secret. And your Father, who sees in secret, will repay you.

"And when you pray, do not be like the hypocrites who love to stand and pray in synagogues and on the street corners, so that others might see them. In truth, I tell you, they already have their reward. But when you pray go to your private space, and lock your door, and there pray to your Father. Your Father, who sees what is secret, will repay you. And when you pray, do not rattle on like the pagans do, thinking they will get a hearing because of the multiplicity of their words. No, do not pray like that. Your heavenly Father already knows what you need.

"This is how you are to pray:

"Our Father in heaven,
hallowed be your name,
your kingdom come,
your will be done on earth, as it is in heaven.
Give us this day our daily bread;
and forgive us our debts, as we forgive who are in debt to us.
And put us not to the test, but protect us from the evil one.

"If you forgive others their offenses, your heavenly Father will forgive you yours. But, if you do not forgive others, neither will your heavenly Father forgive you your offenses.

"When you fast, do not look gloomy like the hypocrites do. They put on long and drawn faces, so that people can tell they are fasting. In truth, I tell you, they already have their reward. But, when you fast, anoint your head and wash your face, so that you may not appear to be fasting, except to your Father who is in heaven. And your Father who sees what is hidden will repay you.

"Do not store up treasures for yourselves on earth, where moth and worm can destroy, and thieves can break in and steal. But store up treasures for yourselves in heaven, when moth and worm cannot destroy, nor can thieves break in and steal. For where your treasure is there will your heart also be.

"The lamp of the body is the eye. If the eye is sound, the whole body will be filled with light, but if your eye is bad, your whole body will be filled with darkness. And if the light in you is darkness, how great will be that darkness.

"No one can serve two masters. Either he will hate the one and love the other, or respect the one and despise the other. You cannot serve God and money.

"And so, I tell you, do not worry about your life, what you will eat or drink, nor about your body and how you will clothe it. Is not life more than food and the body more than clothing? Look at the birds of the air; they do not sow nor reap, nor do they gather into barns. Your heavenly Father feeds them. Are you not worth much more than they? Can any of you with all your worrying extend his life by a single moment? Why are you anxious about clothes? Look at the flowers in the field; they neither sew nor spin, yet not even Solomon in all his glorious array was ever clothed like one of them. If God so clothes the grass of the field, which today flourishes and tomorrow is thrown into the oven, will he not care much more for you, O you of little faith?

"So do not worry, and do not say 'What are we to eat?' or 'What are we to drink?' or 'What are we to wear?' All these things the pagans seek. Your heavenly Father knows you need all these things. Set your hearts on the kingdom first, and all these things will be added to you besides. Worry no longer, little flock, for your father is pleased to give you the kingdom. Sell your possessions, give to the poor, and provide moneybags for yourselves that do not wear out, an inexhaustible treasure in heaven, which no thief can find, and no moths can destroy. For where your treasure is, so also is your heart. So do not worry about tomorrow; tomorrow will take care of itself. Sufficient for the day is the trouble it bears."

While he was speaking, some people present told him about the Galileans whose blood Pilate mingled with the blood of the sacrifices. He said to them, "Do you think that because these Galileans suffered this shame they were worse sinners than other Galileans? Not at all! But I tell you, if you do not change your ways, you will all perish as they did. Or again, those eighteen people who were crushed when the tower at Siloam fell on them, do you think they were more guilty than the other inhabitants of Jerusalem? Not at all! But I tell you: unless you change your ways, you will all perish the way they did."

He then told them a parable. "There was once a man who had a fig tree planted in his orchard. When he came to collect the fruit, he found none. He told the gardener, 'For three years now I have come to collect fruit from this tree, but I have found none. Cut it down. Why should it just waste good land?' The gardener said to him, 'Sir, let it stand for one more year. I will dig up the soil and fertilize it, then, perhaps, it will bear fruit in the future. If not, then cut it down.'"

Then Jesus told the crowd, "Prepare yourselves! Fasten your belts and light your torches, and be like servants waiting for their master's return from a wedding. Be ready to open immediately when he comes and knocks. Fortunate are those servants whom the master finds ready on his arrival. In truth, I say to you, he will fasten his robe around him, have them recline at table, and proceed to wait on them. And if he should come in the second or third watch and find them alert, truly blessed will be those servants. But you can be sure of this, if the master of the house had known the hour when the thief was coming, he would not have let his house be broken into. So must you also be prepared, for at an hour you do not expect, the Son of Man will come."

Then Peter said, "Lord, is this parable meant for us or for everyone?" Jesus replied, "Who, then, is the faithful and prudent servant whom the master will put in charge of his servants to give them their food at the proper times? Blessed is that servant whom the master, on arriving, finds hard at work. In truth, I tell you, he will put him in charge of all his property.

"But if that servant says to himself, 'My master is delayed in coming,' and begins to beat the manservants and maidservants, to eat and drink and get drunk, then the master will come at an unexpected day and hour and will punish him severely and treat him as disloyal and untrustworthy. That servant who knew his master's will but made no preparations and did not follow his master's instructions will be beaten severely. The servant who was ignorant of his master's will but acted in a way deserving of severe punishment shall be beaten only lightly. Much will be required of the one who is given much, and even more will be demanded of the one who is entrusted with more.

"I have come to bring a fire to the earth, and how I wish it were already blazing! There is a baptism with which I am to be baptized, and how great is my impatience for it to be accomplished. Do you think I have come to bring peace?

"Do not judge and you will not be judged. How you judge others will be the way you will be judged. And the way you measure out to others will be the way it will be measured out to you. Why do you notice the speck in your brother's eye but miss the beam in your own eye? How can you say to your brother 'Let me remove the speck from your eye' while there is a wooden beam in your own eye? You hypocrite, remove the beam from your own eye first, then you will be able to see clearly to remove the speck from your brother's eye.

"Do not give what is holy to dogs, and do not cast pearls to swine, lest they trample them, then turn on you and tear you to pieces.

"Ask, and it will be given to you; search, and you will find; knock, and the door will be opened to you. For everyone who asks will always receive; everyone who searches will eventually find; and everyone who knocks will always have the door opened for him. Is there a man among you who would give his son a stone when he asks for bread, or would give him a snake when he asks for a fish? If those who are evil know how to give good gifts to their children, how much more so will your heavenly Father give good gifts to those who ask him?

"Do to others as you would have them do to you! Do this and you will observe the law and the prophets.

"Enter through the narrow gate. The gate is wide and so is the path that leads to destruction. Many go that way. The road that leads to life is narrow, and so is the gate at the end of that road. Few there are who find it.

"Beware of false prophets who come to you dressed in sheep's clothing but in reality are ravenous wolves. Their fruit will strip away their mask. Do people pick grapes from thorn bushes? Or figs from thistles? Likewise, a healthy tree will produce good fruit, but a rotten tree can produce only bad fruit. A healthy tree cannot produce bad fruit, nor can a rotten tree produce good fruit. Any tree that does not produce good fruit is cut down and thrown into the fire. You brood of vipers, how can your speech be good when you yourselves are evil, for words flow out from one's heart. Good things come from hearts filled with goodness; only evil can come from a heart that is rotten. I tell you again, people will judge you by your fruits. So I tell you now, for every hurtful and reckless word people utter, they will account for on the Day of Judgment. It is by your words you will be justified, and by your words you will be condemned."

Some of the scribes and Pharisees spoke up. "Teacher, we would like to see your credentials, a sign from you that you are authorized to speak and do the things you do."

"An evil and faithless generation demands a sign, do you? The only sign you will be given is the sign of the prophet Jonah. As Jonah was in the belly of the whale for three days and three nights, so the Son of Man will rest in the belly of the earth for three days and three nights. On the Day of Judgment the men of Nineveh [a pagan town that repented when told God would punish them for their evil ways] will stand up and bear witness against this generation for its condemnation. For, when Jonah preached to them, they repented. And I tell you, one greater than Jonah is here.

"On Judgment Day, the Queen of the South will appear and give evidence against this generation, because she came from the ends of the earth to listen to the wisdom of Solomon, and yet there is something greater than Solomon here.

"When an evil spirit leaves someone, it wanders through parched areas, looking for a place to rest. Finding none, it returns to the place it has left. Finding it swept clean, and in good order, it goes out and gathers other spirits more evil than itself, and they return and establish themselves there, so the person's situation is worse than before. So it will be with this generation.

"Not everyone who says to me 'Lord, Lord' will enter the kingdom of heaven, only the ones who do the will of my Father in heaven. When the time comes, there will be many saying to me, 'Lord, Lord, did we not prophesy in your name? Did we not cast out devils in your name? Did we not perform miracles in your name?' Then I will say to them, 'Away from me, you frauds. You did not know me then; I do not know you now.'

"In short, anyone who listens to these words and acts on them will be like the sensible man who built his house on solid ground. The rains came, the floods rose, the winds blew hard against that house, but it did not fall. It was built on solid ground. But everyone who listens to these words and does not act on them is like the stupid man who built his house on sand. The rains came, the floods rose, the wind blew hard against that house, and it fell. And what a fall it had!"

Jesus finished his discourse, and his words made a deep impression on the people, because he taught with authority, and not like the scribes (who merely dabbled in opinions).

SIX

After he had come down from the mountain, large crowds followed him. A leper approached him, bowed down in front of him, and said, "Lord, if it is in your heart, you can cure me." Jesus stretched out his hand, touched him, and, saying to him, "I do wish you to be cured," the man was healed immediately. Jesus strictly forbade him to tell anyone, but to show himself to the priest, and make the offering prescribed by Moses, as proof of his cure.

When Jesus entered Capernaum, a centurion (a Roman officer in charge of a hundred soldiers) came up to him and pleaded with him; "Sir, my servant is lying at home paralyzed, and suffering greatly."

"I will come down and cure him," Jesus said.

"Sir," the centurion replied, "I am not worthy that you should come to my house. Merely give the word, and my servant will be healed. For I am under authority myself, and I have soldiers under me. If I say to one, 'Go,' he goes. If I say to another, 'Come,' he comes. And if I say to my servant, 'Do this,' he does it."

When Jesus heard this, he was astonished, and said to those standing around, "I have not found such great faith in all of Israel. And I tell you, many will come from the east and the west to take their places with Abraham, Isaac, and Jacob at the feast in the kingdom of heaven, but the children of the kingdom will be turned away into the darkness outside, where there will be wailing and grinding of teeth." Then Jesus said to the centurion, "Go back home! As you have believed, so it will be done to you." At that very hour the servant was healed.

Entering Peter's house, he found Peter's mother-in-law lying in bed with a fever. He touched her hand, the fever left her, and she got up and began to wait on them. When it was evening, they brought to him all who were possessed by devils. With one word he drove them out, and cured all the sick as well, thus fulfilling the prophecy of Isaiah, "He took away our diseases and bore our infirmities."

As crowds began to gather, Jesus gave orders for his disciples to leave for the other side of the lake. Then he got into the boat, followed by his disciples. Suddenly a violent storm came down upon the lake, with the waves rushing over the boat. Jesus was asleep. They went to him and woke him. "Save us, Lord," they said to him, "we are sinking."

He said to them, "Why are you so frightened, men of little faith?" With that he stood up and rebuked the wind and the sea, and all became calm. The men were astounded and remarked, "What kind of man is this that even the wind and the sea obey him?"

When he came to the other side, to the country of the Gadarenes, two possessed men came rushing out of the tombs at him. They were of such terrifying appearance that people would not pass by there. They stood shouting at Jesus, "What do you want of us, Son of God. Have you come here to torture us before the appointed time?" Now, some distance away from there was a large herd of swine feeding. The evil spirits pleaded with him, "If you intend to drive us out, send us into that herd of pigs." "Go, then," he said to them. They came out of the men and entered the swine, driving them headlong over the cliff and into the sea, where the whole herd drowned.

The swineherds fled into the town. When they arrived, they reported everything, including what had happened to the possessed men. The whole town promptly came out to meet Jesus, and begged him to leave their district.

Entering a boat, he made the crossing and arrived at his own town (Capernaum). While there, people brought to him a paralyzed man lying on a stretcher. When Jesus saw their faith, he said to the paralyzed man, "Courage, child, your sins are forgiven." At that, some of the scribes said to themselves, "This man is blaspheming." Jesus knew their thoughts, so he said to them, "Why do you nurture evil thoughts. Which is easier, to say 'Your sins are forgiven' or to say 'Get up and walk'? But that you may know that the Son of Man has authority on earth to forgive sins," he then said to the paralyzed man, "Rise, pick up your stretcher and go home." He rose and went home. When the crowds saw this, they were struck with awe and glorified God who had given such power to men.

Just before the Jewish Passover (the feast commemorating the freeing of the Israelites from slavery in Egypt), Jesus went up to Jerusalem. Entering the temple courtyard, he found people selling cattle and sheep and doves, and moneychangers there to do business. Making a whip out of cords, he drove them all out of the temple precincts, cattle and the sheep as well, and toppled the tables of the moneychangers, scattering their coins across the pavement. To those selling doves, he told them, "Get these things out of here, and stop making my Father's house a marketplace." Then the disciples remembered the words of scripture: "Zeal for your house will consume me." The Judeans (the political leaders) confronted Jesus, demanding, "What proof of authority can you give us to justify what you have done?"

Jesus answered, "Destroy this temple, and in three days I will raise it up." The Jews replied, "It took forty-six years to build this temple, and you will rebuild it in three days?" Jesus was referring to the temple of his body. And when he was raised from the dead, his disciples remembered that he had said this, and they came to believe the scripture and the word Jesus had spoken.

While in Jerusalem for the celebration of Passover, many came to believe in his name when they saw the signs he was performing. Jesus, however, knew them all, and did not trust himself to them, because he knew what was in them. He needed no experts to tell him about human nature. He knew well what was in the human heart.

There was a Pharisee named Nicodemus, a Judean leader, who came to Jesus by night and said to him, "Teacher, we know that you are a teacher who comes from God, for no one could work the signs you do unless God was with him."

Jesus answered, "In truth, I say to you, no one can arrive at the kingdom of God unless he is born from above."

Nicodemus answered, "How can an old man be born again? Surely he cannot reenter his mother's womb and be born a second time, can he?"

"In truth, I tell you," Jesus replied, "no one can enter the kingdom of God without being born of water and the Spirit. What is born of flesh is flesh, what is born of spirit is spirit. Do not be shocked that I tell you, you must be born from above. The wind blows where it wills and you can hear the sound it makes, but from where it comes and where it goes you do not know. So it is with everyone who is born of the Spirit."

"How can this be possible?" Nicodemus answered.

Jesus replied, "You are a teacher in Israel and you do not understand. I tell you truthfully we speak of what we know and we testify about what we have seen, but your people do not accept our testimony. If I tell you about earthly things and you do not believe, how will you believe if I tell you about heavenly things? No one goes up to heaven except the one who has come down from heaven, the Son of Man. And just as Moses lifted up the serpent in the desert [all who looked up at the bronze serpent Moses placed on a pole were healed of their poisonous snakebites] so must the Son of Man be lifted up so that everyone who believes in him will have eternal life.

"For God so loved the world, that he gave his only Son, so that everyone who believes in him might not be lost, but might have eternal life. God sent his Son into the world not to condemn the world, but so that through him the world might be saved. No one who believes in him will be condemned, but whoever refuses to believe is condemned already, because he has refused to believe in the name of God's only Son. And upon this is the judgment that, God has

sent his light into the world, and people have chosen darkness to the light, because their motives are evil. Indeed,
everyone who does evil hates the light and avoids it for fear
that his evil deeds might be exposed. The man, however,
who lives honestly works in broad daylight so that it might
be clearly seen that what he does he does in God."

SEVEN

When Jesus learned that the Pharisees had
heard that he was making and baptizing more disciples than
John (although Jesus himself was not baptizing, only his
disciples), he left Judea. John was arrested at that time, and
Jesus quickened his steps toward Galilee, passing through
towns and villages along the way, and preaching the good
news of the kingdom and healing the sick and those possessed by evil spirits.

On his way to Galilee he had to pass through Samaria,
and came to a town called Sychar, which was near the plot of
land that Jacob had given to his son Joseph. Jacob's well was
there. Jesus, tired from his journey, sat down by the well. It

was about the sixth hour (noontime). A Samaritan woman came to draw water. Jesus said to her, "Woman, would you give me a drink?" His disciples had gone into town to buy food. The Samaritan woman said to him, "What, you a Judean asking me, a Samaritan, for a drink?" Judeans were forbidden by law to associate with Samaritans.

Jesus replied, "If you only knew the honor God is paying you, and who it is who is asking you for a drink, you would ask him, and he would give you living water."

"Sir, you do not have a bucket, and this well is deep; where, then, will you get this living water? Are you greater than our father Jacob, who gave us this well and drank from it himself with his children and his flocks?"

Jesus answered, and said to her, "Everyone who drinks this water will become thirsty again. But whoever drinks the water I give will never again be thirsty. The water I give will become like a well springing up from within to eternal life."

"Sir," the woman said, "give me of this water so I can quench my thirst and not have to keep coming here to draw water."

"Go, and call your husband," Jesus told her, "and come back here."

"I do not have a husband," the woman replied.

"You are right in saying you do not have a husband," Jesus responded. "You have had five husbands and the man you are with now is not your husband. You have spoken truthfully."

"Sir, I perceive you are a prophet," the woman said. "Our fathers worshiped on this mountain, while you say that Jerusalem is the place where people must worship."

"Believe me, woman," Jesus answered, "the time is coming when you will worship the Father neither on this mountain nor in Jerusalem. You worship what you do not know; we worship what we know, for salvation comes from the Judeans. But the hour is coming, and is, indeed, already here, when true worshipers will worship the Father in their hearts and in their lives. That is the kind of worshiper the Father wants. God is spirit and those who worship must worship in their spirit and in the way they live their lives."

"I know that the Messiah is coming," the woman continued, "and when he comes he will tell us everything."

Jesus answered her, "I who am speaking to you am he."

At that point his disciples returned, and were surprised to find him speaking to a woman, though none of them asked, "What do you want with her?" or "Why are you talking with her?"

The woman, in the meantime, put down her water jar and rushed back to the town to tell the people, "Come, and see a man who has told me about everything I ever did. Could he not be the Messiah?"

The people left the town and went out to meet him.

The disciples offered Jesus some food. "Master, take something to eat," they said to him.

"I have food of which you do not know" was his response, which made the disciples ask one another, "Has someone brought him food?"

But Jesus said, "My food is to do the will of my Father who sent me, and to complete his work. Do you not have a saying, 'Four months and then the harvest?' Well, I tell you, look around you and see the fields; they are already ripe for the harvest. The reaper is already collecting his pay as he gathers in the crops for eternal life. The sower and the reaper are celebrating together. And here the proverb proves true, 'One sows, another reaps.' I sent you to harvest that for which you did not labor. Others worked for it and you share the rewards."

Many Samaritans came to believe in him on account of the woman's testimony. "He told me about everything I have ever done." So when they went out to meet Jesus, they asked him to spend some time in their town. He did stay two days, and after speaking to them, many more came to believe in him. They then said to the woman, "We believe no longer because you told us but because we have listened to him ourselves and have come to realize he is the savior of the world."

After staying there for the two days, he continued on his journey to Galilee, where he had the previous experience that led him to comment that a prophet is never accepted in his own country. However, on this journey he was well received by the Galileans, having seen all that he had done in

Jerusalem at the time of the festival, which they had attended.

Stopping at Cana in Galilee, where he had changed the water into wine, a court official whose son was ill at Capernaum approached Jesus. He had heard that Jesus had arrived in Galilee from Judea, so he went and asked Jesus if he would come and cure his son, who was close to death.

"Why is it that people do not believe unless they see signs and wonders?" Jesus commented.

"Sir," the official pressed him, "come down before my son dies."

"Go home," Jesus told him, "your son will live."

The royal official believed what Jesus said to him, and started on his way back home. On the way, his servants met him with the news that the boy had recovered.

The official asked at what time he began to recover. "The fever left him yesterday at the seventh hour" (one o'clock in the afternoon). The father then realized that it was at that exact time that Jesus said "Your son will recover." He and his entire household believed. That was the second sign Jesus worked on his return from Judea to Galilee.

Jesus then wandered through the surrounding villages, teaching along the way. Summoning the Twelve, he sent them out two by two, giving them authority over evil spirits, and to cure diseases, and instructing them to take nothing for the journey except a staff; no food, no traveling bag, no money in their purses, and no spare clothes. "Do not go into pagan territory, and do not enter Samaritan towns. Go instead to the lost sheep of the house of Israel and proclaim to them that the kingdom of heaven is fast approaching. Cure the sick, raise the dead, heal the lepers, and drive out devils. You received without charge, give without charge." So they went out and preached repentance, and cast out many devils, and anointed many sick people with oil and cured them.

"I tell you, beware of people, they will hand you over to courts and flog you in their synagogues. You will be brought before governors and kings because of me, so you can bear witness to me before the world. But do not be afraid either of what you will say or how you will say it. What you are to say will be given to you when that time comes, for it will not be you who is speaking, but the Spirit your Father will be speaking through you.

"Brother will turn over his own brother to death, and father his own child. Children will betray their own parents and have them put to death. You will be despised by all because of me, but he who perseveres to the end will be saved. If they persecute you in your own town, flee to the next. If they persecute you in that town, flee to another. In all honesty, I tell you, you will not have exhausted all the towns in Israel before the Son of Man comes.

"No disciple is above his teacher; no slave his master. It

is enough for a disciple to become like his teacher, and for the slave to become like his master. If they malign the master of the house with the name Beelzebul, will they not malign his servants even more? So do not be afraid of them. Whatever is now covered up will be brought out into the open, and whatever has been kept hidden will be exposed. What I say to you in the dark, tell it in broad daylight; what you hear in whispers, shout from the housetops.

"Do not be afraid of those who can kill the body; they cannot kill the soul. Fear the One who can kill both body and soul in hell. Can you not buy two sparrows for a penny apiece? Yet not one falls to the ground without your Father knowing about it. Know that every hair of your head is accounted for, so do not be afraid, for you are worth more than many sparrows.

"I tell you further, if anyone acknowledges me before others, that person will I acknowledge before my Father in heaven. But if anyone denies me before others, that person will I deny before my Father in heaven. I have come to set fire to the earth, and how I wish it were already blazing! There is a baptism with which I must be baptized, and how impatient I am for it to be accomplished! Do not think that my coming will bring peace upon earth. No, I tell you. My coming will not bring peace, but a sword. My coming will set son against father, daughter against mother, daughter-in-law against mother-in-law. Indeed, a person's enemies will be the members of his own household.

"No one who prefers father or mother before me is worthy of me. No one who prefers son or daughter before me is worthy of me. Anyone who does not take up his cross and follow me is not worthy of me. Anyone who finds his life will lose it, and anyone who loses his life for my sake will find it. Anyone who welcomes you, welcomes me; and anyone who welcomes me, welcomes the One who sent me. Anyone who welcomes a prophet because he is a prophet will have a prophet's reward. Anyone who welcomes a righteous person because he is righteous will have the reward for receiving a righteous person. If anyone so much as gives a cup of cold water to one of these little ones because he is a disciple, let me tell you, that person most certainly will not go without his reward."

EIGHT

After instructing the twelve apostles, Jesus continued on his tour of the towns, teaching and preaching along the way.

One day, on a sabbath, Jesus went to dinner at the home of a leading Pharisee. The guests were watching him closely. In front of him was a man who had dropsy. Jesus asked the Pharisees and the experts in the law, "Is it lawful to cure on the sabbath?" They said nothing. So Jesus took the man, and, after healing him, told him to leave. Then he said to the dinner guests, "Who among you, if your son, or even your ox or ass, falls into a cistern, would not immediately pull him out on the sabbath?" But they were unable to give him an answer.

He then told a parable to the invited guests, noticing how they were maneuvering for the choice seats at table. "When you are invited to a wedding feast, do not recline in the place of honor. A guest more distinguished than yourself may have been invited by the host, who may then approach you and say, 'Give your place to this man.' Then, embarrassed, you will have to take the lowest place. Rather, when you are invited, go and take the lowest place, so that when the host comes to you, he may say, 'Go and take a higher place.' Then you will rise in the esteem of the other guests at table. For everyone who exalts himself will be humbled, but the one who humbles himself will be honored."

Then he said to the host who invited him, "When you have a lunch or dinner, do not invite family or the wealthy and distinguished, for they will invite you in return. Rather, when you throw a banquet, invite the poor, the crippled, the lame, the blind. Blessed will you be because they have no way of repaying you. You will be richly repaid at the resurrection of the just."

One of the other guests, hearing what Jesus said, replied, "Blessed are those who will dine in the kingdom of God!"

Jesus responded, "A man threw a great banquet and invited many. As the time of the banquet approached, he sent his servants to remind those invited, 'Come, everything is now ready.' One by one they all excused themselves. The first one said, 'Pray, hold me excused, for I have bought a field and I must go to examine it.' Another said, 'Pray, hold me excused, I have just bought five yoke of oxen, and I must go and examine them.' Another said, 'Pray, hold me excused, I just married a woman, and I cannot come.'

"The servant reported all this to his master. He went into a rage and ordered his servant, 'Go out into the back roads and into the hamlets and invite everyone you see, the poor, the crippled, the blind, and the lame, and make them come in, so that my house may be full. For I tell you not one of those invited will ever eat at my table or taste of my feast.' "

John, meanwhile, had heard in prison what the Messiah was doing and sent his disciples to ask him, "Are you the One who is to come, or should we look for another?" Jesus' response was "Go back and tell John what you have seen and heard: The blind see, the crippled walk, lepers are cleansed, the deaf hear, the dead are raised to life, and the poor have the good news preached to them, and blessed are they who are not scandalized by my ways."

As the men were leaving, Jesus spoke to the people about John. "What did you go out to the desert to see? A reed swaying with the breeze? No? Then, what did you go out to see? A man wearing fine clothes? I tell you, those who wear fine clothes are found in the houses of kings. Then, what did you go out to see? Was it a prophet? Yes, I tell you, and much more than a prophet. It is he of whom scripture says: 'Behold, I am sending my messenger ahead of you to prepare the way before you.'

"I tell you, of all the children born of women, there is no one greater than John the baptizer, and yet the least in the kingdom of heaven is greater than he. Since John came, up to the present, the kingdom of heaven has been stormed by violence, and the violent are seizing it by force. Because it was toward John and the events surrounding him the prophecies and the law were pointing, and, if you are open to accepting it, he is the Elijah whom you have been expecting to return. If you have ears that hear, heed this message!

"How can I find a comparison to this generation? It is like a group of children complaining to their playmates, 'We have piped happy tunes to you and you would not dance. We sang dirges and you would not mourn.' For John came neither eating nor drinking, and you say he is possessed by an evil spirit. The Son of Man came eating and drinking and you say, 'Behold, a glutton, a drunkard, a companion of tax collectors [extortioners in their day] and sinners [mostly those expelled from the religion]. So, think of it, wisdom is proven by her accomplishments.' "

Then Jesus suddenly exclaimed loudly, "I thank you, Father, Lord of heaven and earth, for having hidden these things from the learned and the clever, and making them believable to the childlike. Yes, Father, for it so pleased you. My Father has entrusted everything to me, and no one

68

knows the Father but the Son and those to whom the Son wishes to reveal him.

"All you who are weary and heavily burdened, come to me, and I will give you rest. Take upon yourselves my yoke, and learn from me, for I am gentle and humble of heart, and you will find rest for your souls. You will learn that my yoke is easy and my burden light."

Knowing the scribes and Pharisees were plotting against him, he withdrew from the district. Many followed him, and he cured them all, but warned them to tell no one. In doing these things he was fulfilling the words of the prophet Isaiah; "Behold, my servant whom I have chosen, my beloved, in whom I take delight. I will send my Spirit upon him, and he will preach righteousness to the Gentiles [non-Israelite people, who did not know their God]. He will not be contentious or rowdy, nor will his voice be heard in the streets. He will not break a fragile reed, or snuff out a flickering lamp, until he has brought righteousness to victory. In him all peoples will place their hope."

One sabbath day, while he was preaching in a synagogue, there was a woman present who had been crippled by an evil spirit for eighteen years. She was bent over, and totally incapable of standing up straight. When Jesus saw her he called to her and said, "Woman, you are now free of your affliction." He laid his hands on her and she at once stood up straight, and praised God. The leader of the synagogue, however, was indignant and told the congregation,

"There are six days when work should be done. Come on those days to be cured, not on the sabbath."

The Lord said to him, "Hypocrites! Does not each of you on the sabbath untie his ox or his ass from the manger, and lead it out to the water. This daughter of Abraham, whom Satan has held bound for eighteen years, should she not be untied from her bondage on the sabbath."

As Jesus traveled from one village to another, preaching and proclaiming the good news of the kingdom of God, the Twelve accompanied him.

There were also some women who had been cured of evil spirits and infirmities who also accompanied them. Among them was Mary, called Magdalene, from whom he had cast out seven devils; Joanna, the wife of Herod's steward, Chusa; Susanna; and many others who provided for their needs out of their own resources.

One day, Jesus was sitting by the shore of the lake. Soon, a huge crowd gathered around him, so he got into one of the boats and sat there. The people stayed on the shore while Jesus spoke to them about many things in parables. He said, "Listen to me carefully, a sower went out to sow. As he sowed, some seeds fell on the pathway. The birds came and ate them up. Others fell among rocks, where they had little soil. They sprang up at once, but because they had little soil, the sun scorched them, and having no roots, they withered and died. Others fell among thorns. The thorns grew up and choked them. Others fell on rich soil and produced a rich crop, some a hundred fold, others sixty fold, and others thirty fold. Those of you who have ears, heed what I have said."

The disciples approached him and asked, "Why do you talk to them in parables?" He replied, "To you is granted to know the mysteries of the kingdom, but to them it is not granted. Anyone who has and is open to receive will be given more, and will have even more than his share. Anyone who does not have and is not open to receive will lose even what he thinks he possesses. The reason I speak to them in parables is that they look without seeing, and listen without hearing or understanding, thus fulfilling the prophecy of Isaiah; 'You shall listen but not understand. You shall look but not see. Dense is the heart of this people. They have dulled their ears and closed their eyes, lest they see with their eyes and hear with their ears, and understand with their heart and turn to me, and I heal them.' But blessed are your eyes, because they see, and blessed are your ears, because they hear. I tell you, many prophets and good people longed to see what you see and never saw it; to hear what you hear and never heard it.

"Let me explain to you, then, the parable of the sower. The seed sown on the path is the one who hears the word of the kingdom but is not open to understanding. The evil one comes and steals what was sown in his heart. The seed sown on rocky ground is the one who listens to the word and accepts it at once with joy. But he has no root and does not last. When some trial or persecution comes because of the word, he falls away at once. The seed sown among thorns is the one who hears the word, but worldly concerns or love of money choke the word, so it produces nothing. But the seed sown on rich soil is the one who hears the word, is open to understanding it, bears fruit a hundred or sixty or thirty fold."

He told them another parable. "The kingdom of heaven is like a man who sowed good seed in his field. While everyone was asleep, his enemy came and sowed weeds all throughout the wheat, then ran off. When the wheat sprouted and grew, the weeds appeared along with it. The owner's servants went to him and said, 'Master, did you not sow good seed in your field? There are weeds as well; where could they have come from?' 'An enemy has done this,' he said. The servants asked him, 'Shall we pull up the weeds?' 'No,' he said. 'If you do that, you will pull up the wheat as well. Let them both grow together. Then, at harvest time I will tell the reapers, "First collect the weeds, tie them in bundles to be burned. Then gather the wheat and put it in my barn." ' "

He offered them another parable. "The kingdom of heaven is like a mustard seed which a man took and sowed in his field. It is the tiniest of seeds, but when it grows it is the biggest of the bushes, so that flocks of birds come and dwell in its branches."

He told them still another parable. "The kingdom of

heaven is like yeast which a woman took and mixed with three measures of flour until the whole batch was leavened."

This was the way Jesus spoke to them, in parables. And, indeed, he would speak to them in no way other than parables, fulfilling what was said through the prophet (Isaiah); "I will open my mouth in parables. I will announce things that have been hidden since the foundation of the world."

Then, walking away from the crowd, he went into the house. The disciples came up to him and said, "Explain to us the parable of the weeds in the field." He replied, "He who sows good seed is the Son of Man, the field is the world, the good seed are the children of the kingdom. The weeds are the children of the evil one, and the enemy who sows them is the devil. The harvest is the end of the world, and the harvesters are the angels. Just as weeds are gathered up and burned, so will it be at the end of the world. The Son of Man will send his angels. They will gather from around his kingdom all those who lead others into sin and all evildoers. They will throw them into the fiery furnace, where there will be wailing and grinding of teeth. The righteous, on the other hand, will shine like the sun in the kingdom of their Father. Those who have ears to hear had better listen.

"Again, the kingdom of heaven is like a treasure buried in a field, which someone finds, and immediately hides. Overjoyed, he goes off, sells everything he owns, and buys the field. Or, the kingdom of heaven can be likened to a merchant in search of fine pearls. When he finds one really valuable pearl, he goes, sells all his possessions, and buys it. Or again, the kingdom of heaven is like a net thrown into the sea that collects all kinds of things. When it is full, the fishermen haul it ashore, sit down, and begin to sort out everything. What is good they throw into buckets, and what is no good they throw away.

"This is how it will be at the end of the world. The angels will go and separate the wicked from the good, and throw them into the raging fire, where there will be wailing and grinding of teeth. Do you understand all that I have said?"

"Yes," they responded.

And he said further, "Every scribe instructed in the kingdom of heaven is like the master of the house who brings from his storehouse both the new and the old."

When Jesus finished telling these parables, he departed from there.

NINE

It was around that time that Herod had arrested John, bound him, and put him in prison, on account of Herodias, the wife of his brother Philip, for John had said to him, "It is not lawful for you to have her." Herodias was violently angry with John and wanted to kill him but was unable. Although Herod also wanted to kill him, he was afraid of the people; they regarded him as a prophet. He also feared John, knowing him to be a righteous man and a holy man, so he protected him from harm. When he heard him speak he was very much perplexed, yet he liked to listen to him. But at Herod's birthday celebration, Herodias had her opportunity. At the banquet were the courtiers, the military officers, and the leading men of Galilee. Herodias' daughter danced before all the guests, which pleased Herod so much that he swore to give her anything she asked, even if it be half his kingdom. She went to her mother and told her what the king had promised. Prompted by her mother, she hurried back to the king and said, "Give me the head of John the baptizer here on a platter."

The king was sorely distressed, but, because of the oath and the guests who were present, he ordered that it be done, so he had John beheaded in the prison. His head was brought on a dish and given to the girl, who then took it to her mother. John's disciples came and took the body and buried it, then went and told Jesus.

At that time Jesus was speaking to the crowds, and the apostles had just returned from their missionary journey and were sharing with Jesus and one another what they had done and taught. Hearing of John's death, he said to the apostles, "Come away by yourselves to a deserted place and rest awhile." People were coming and going in such numbers, they had no opportunity even to eat. So they withdrew by boat across the Sea of Galilee to a deserted place by themselves. When the crowds heard of this, they followed on foot from their towns. When he reached shore and stepped out of the boat, he saw the vast crowd before him. Moved to pity for them, he healed their sick.

When evening approached, his disciples came to him and said, "This is a deserted place and the day is almost over. Why not dismiss the crowd so they can go to the villages and buy food for themselves." Jesus replied, "There is no need for them to do that. You give them something to eat."

But they answered, "We have only five loaves and two fish. What is that among so many?"

"Bring them here to me!" he said. Then he gave orders for the people to recline in groups on the green grass. So they sat down in groups of fifty and a hundred. Then, taking the five loaves and the two fish, he raised his eyes to heaven and said the blessing. Breaking the loaves, he gave them to his disciples, who gave them to the crowds. They all ate as much as they wanted. They then collected what was left over, enough to fill twelve baskets. Those who ate were about five thousand men, not counting the women and children.

When the people saw the sign that he had done, they said, "This is indeed the prophet who is to come into the world." When Jesus realized they would try to take him by force and make him king, he told the apostles to get into the boat, and he himself withdrew alone to the mountain to pray.

When it was evening, he was there alone. The boat, meanwhile, was a few miles offshore, and because of the strong headwinds, and the waves tossing it about, was unable to make any headway. During the fourth watch of the night (between three and six A.M.), Jesus came toward them, walking on the sea. When the disciples saw him walking on the sea, they were terrified. "It is a ghost," they said as they cried out in sheer fright.

Jesus called to them, "Take courage, it is I. Do not be afraid!"

Peter said to him, "If it is you, Lord, tell me to come to you on the water."

"Come," Jesus replied.

Peter climbed out of the boat and began walking toward Jesus, but when he realized how strong the wind was, he panicked and began to sink. Crying out, he said, "Save me, Lord." Jesus reached out and took him by the hand, and said to him, "O you of little faith, why did you doubt?" When they both climbed aboard the boat, the wind immediately died down. The disciples were astounded and paid him homage, saying, "You really are the Son of God." They had not understood what had happened to the loaves and the fishes. Their eyes were closed to what had taken place.

After crossing, they arrived at Gennesaret. When the men there recognized him, they sent word to the surrounding countryside. As they passed through their villages along the Gennesaret coast, people brought to him all those who were sick, and begged him to allow them to just touch the tassel on his cloak. When they did so, they were cured.

The next day, the crowd that remained across the sea saw that there had been only one boat there, and that Jesus had not entered the boat with the disciples, but that the disciples had left by themselves. Other boats came from Tiberias near the place where they had eaten the bread when the Lord gave thanks. When the crowd saw that neither Jesus nor his disciples were there, they themselves got into boats and went to Capernaum, looking for Jesus.

When they found him across the sea, they asked him, "Rabbi, when did you come here?" Jesus said to them, "In truth, I tell you, you are looking for me, not because you saw signs, but because you ate the loaves and were filled. Do not spend your energy looking for food that perishes, but for the food that endures for eternal life, which the Son of Man will give you. For on him the Father, God, has set His seal." They said to him, "What can we do to accomplish the works of God?" Jesus answered, "This is the work of God, that you believe in the one He sent." They said, "What sign can you perform that we may believe in you? What can you do? Our ancestors ate manna in the wilderness, as it is written, 'Bread from heaven he gave them to eat.' "

Jesus said to them, "In truth, I tell you, it was not Moses who gave the bread from heaven; my Father gives you the true bread from heaven. For the bread of God is that which has come down from heaven and gives life to the world."

They said to him, "Sir, give us this bread always." Jesus said to them, "I am the bread of life; whoever comes to me will never hunger, and whoever believes in me will never thirst. But I told you already that although you have seen me you do not believe. Everything that the Father gives me will come to me, and I will not turn away anyone who comes to me, because I came down from heaven not to do my will, but to do the will of the One who sent me. And this is the will of the One who sent me, that I should not lose anything of what He gave me, but that I should raise it up on the last day. This is the will of my Father, that everyone who sees the Son and believes in him may have eternal life, and I shall raise him up on the last day."

The Judean people complained because he said, "I am the bread that has come down from heaven," and they said, "Is this not Jesus, the son of Joseph? Do we not know his father and mother? How then can he say, 'I have come down from heaven'?" Jesus answered, and said to them, "Stop complaining among yourselves. No one can come to me unless the Father who sent me draw him, and I will raise him up on the last day. It is written in the prophets, 'They shall all be taught by God.' Everyone who listens to my Father and learns from Him comes to me. Not that anyone has seen the Father, except the one who is from God; he has seen the Father. In truth, I tell you, whoever believes has eternal life. I am the bread of life. Your ancestors ate manna in the wilderness, and they died. This is the bread that comes down from heaven, and whoever eats it will not die. I am the living bread come down from heaven; whoever eats this bread will live forever, and the bread that I will give is my flesh for the life of the world."

They still argued among themselves, "How can this man give us his flesh to eat?" Jesus responded, "In truth, I tell you, unless you eat the flesh of the Son of Man and drink his blood, you do not have life within you. Whoever eats my flesh and drinks my blood has eternal life, and I will raise him up on the last day, for my flesh is real food and my blood is real drink. Whoever eats my flesh and drinks my blood lives in me and I in him. Just as the living Father sent me and I have life because of the Father, so also the one who feeds on me will have life because of me. This is the bread that has come down from heaven. Not like your ancestors who ate the manna and died, whoever eats this bread will live forever." These things he taught while at the synagogue in Capernaum.

Many of his disciples who were listening said to him, "This is a difficult saying; who can accept it?" Since Jesus knew his disciples were murmuring about this, he said to them, "Does this shock you? What if you were to see the Son of Man ascending to where he was before? It is the spirit that gives life; the flesh is of no import. The words I have spoken to you are spirit and life. But there are even some of you who do not believe." Jesus knew from the beginning the ones who would not believe and the one who would betray him. And he said, "For this reason I have told you that no one can come to me unless it is granted him by my Father."

As a result, many of his disciples returned to their former way of life and no longer accompanied him. Jesus then said to the Twelve, "Do you also want to leave?" Simon Peter spoke up and said, "Lord, to whom shall we go? You have the words of eternal life. We have come to believe and are convinced that you are the Holy One of God." Jesus answered them, "Did I not choose you twelve? Yet is not one of you a devil?" He was referring to Judas, son of Simon the Iscariot; it was he who would betray him, one of the Twelve.

After this Jesus went around from place to place within Galilee. He had no desire to go to Judea, because the Judeans were trying to kill him. Scribes and Pharisees came to Jesus from Jerusalem. They asked him, "Why do your disciples break away from the traditions of our ancestors, and eat food with unwashed hands?" (This was not ordinary washing of hands before eating, but lengthy ritual washings.) Jesus in reply said to them, "And why do you break the commandment of God for the sake of your tradition? For God said, 'Honor your father and your mother,' and 'Whoever curses father or mother will die.' But you say, 'Whoever says to father or mother, "Any money I might have used to support you is now dedicated to God," is no longer obliged to support his father or mother.' You have made null and void God's own command for the sake of your tradition. Hypocrites, well did Isaiah prophesy of you when he said; 'This people honors me with their lips, but their hearts are far from me. Useless is their worship, for they teach as God's law their own human precepts.' "

He then called out to the people and gathered them around him. He explained to them, "It is not what goes into one's mouth that defiles a person; it is what comes out of the mouth that really defiles a person." His disciples walked over to him and said to him, "Do you not know that the Pharisees were offended by what you just said?" He replied, "Leave them alone; they are blind guides of those who enjoy being blind. If a blind person leads blind people, they will all fall into a pit."

Then Peter said to him, "Explain to us that parable!"

"Are even you still without understanding?" he said to them. "Do you not realize that whatever enters the mouth passes into the stomach, and is expelled into the toilet. But the things that come out of the mouth come from the heart, and they are the ones that defile. It is from the heart that come evil thoughts, murder, adultery, uncleanness, theft, false witness, blasphemy. These are the things that defile a person. To eat with unwashed hands does not defile a person."

Jesus then left that area and wandered up into the region of Tyre and Sidon (modern Sur and Sanyda in Lebanon. At that time the people there were generally not believers in the God of the Jews). A Canaanite woman from that region came toward Jesus, shouting, "Have pity on me, Lord, Son of David! My daughter is tormented by an evil spirit." But

Jesus did not respond. His disciples came to him and pleaded with him, "Give her what she wants. She keeps shouting after us."

"I was sent only to the lost sheep of the house of Israel." But the woman approached him, and falling down at his feet, begged him, "Lord, help me." He replied, "It is not right to take the children's food and give it to the family pets." "True," she replied, "but don't the family pets eat the crumbs that fall from their master's table?"

"Woman, you have great faith. Your request is granted." From that very moment her daughter was healed.

Moving on from there, he walked toward Sidon, then south toward the Sea of Galilee, stopping in the area of the Decapolis. As a large crowd was following him, he went up on the hillside and sat down. The crowd brought to him the lame, the blind, the deformed, the mute, and others with various ailments. They placed them at his feet and he cured them. A particular deaf man with a speech impediment was brought to him. They begged Jesus to heal him. Taking the man off to the side away from the crowd, he put his finger into the man's ears. Then, spitting he touched his tongue, and looking up to heaven, groaned, and said to him, *"Eph-phatha."* ("Be opened.") Immediately, the man's ears were opened and his speech impediment was gone, and he spoke clearly. He ordered them to tell no one. But the more he ordered them, the more they proclaimed it. The crowd was amazed to hear the mute speak, see the deformed with straightened limbs, the lame walking, and the blind looking all around. They praised God for his goodness. He has done all things well. He even makes the deaf hear and the mute speak.

As the crowd stayed on day after day, Jesus felt pity for them. He called together his disciples and said to them, "My heart is moved with pity for the people. They have been with us for three days and have nothing to eat. I do not want to send them away hungry, for fear they may collapse on the way."

His disciples said, "Where will we be able to get enough food in this out of the way place to feed such a crowd."

Jesus said to them, "How many loaves do you have?" "Seven," they replied, "and a few fish." He then ordered the crowd to sit on the ground. Taking the seven loaves and the fish, he gave thanks, broke the loaves, and he gave them to his disciples, who then distributed them among the crowd. They all ate till they were filled. Picking up the fragments that were left over, they filled seven baskets. Those who ate were four thousand, not counting the women and children.

Then, dismissing the crowd, he and his disciples climbed into the boat and crossed over to the region of Magadan.

TEN

Pharisees and Sadducees (told by their agents as to Jesus' whereabouts) found Jesus and approached him in an attempt to trap him. (Pharisees, being strict religious Judeans, had little to do with the Sadducees, who were liberal devotees of pagan Greek culture and had all but abandoned traditional Judean beliefs. Seeing the two groups now working together shows the extent of their hostility toward Jesus.) They asked him for a sign from heaven as evidence of God's approval for what he was saying and doing. He said to them in reply, "In the evening you say, 'The sky is red, tomorrow will be a good day.' In the morning you say, 'The

sky is red with heavy clouds, it is going to be stormy.'
Strange, you can read the signs in the sky but cannot read
the signs of the times. An evil and faithless generation demands a sign. I tell you, no sign will be given it other than
the sign of Jonah." He then turned and walked away from
them.

Arriving on the other side of the sea, the disciples remembered they had forgotten to bring bread, and had only
one loaf with them. Jesus said to them, "Beware of the
leaven of the Pharisees and Sadducees." They thought, "It
is because we forgot to bring bread that he is saying that."
Seeing their confusion, he said to them, "You of little faith,
why do you think I said that, because you have no bread?
Do you still not understand? Remember the five loaves and
the five thousand, and how many baskets of leftovers you
picked up? Or the seven loaves and the four thousand, and
how many basketfuls you picked up that day. How come
you do not understand that I was not speaking about
bread? Beware of the leaven of the Pharisees and the Sadducees." Then they understood that he was not speaking
about bread, but about the teachings of the Pharisees and
Sadducees.

Continuing on his journey, he arrived at Bethsaida,
where people brought to him a blind man and begged him
to touch him. He took the blind man by the hand and led
him outside the village. Putting spittle on his eyes, he laid

his hands on him and asked, "Do you see anything?" Looking around, he said, "I see people like trees walking." Then he laid his hands on him a second time, and he saw clearly. His sight was now fully restored and he could see everything distinctly. Then Jesus sent him home, telling him to avoid the village.

While in that village, someone in the crowd said to him, "Teacher, tell my brother to share the inheritance with me." He replied, "Friend, who appointed me as your judge and arbiter?" Then he said to the crowd, "Avoid greed in all its forms, for though you may be rich, it does not assure you of eternal life." Then he told them a parable. "There was a rich man whose farm produced an abundant harvest. He said to himself, 'What shall I do, for I have no room for all this harvest?' Then he said, 'I know what I will do. I will tear down my barns and build larger ones, then I can store all my grain as well as other goods. Then I shall say to myself, "Now you have goods enough for many years, so relax, eat, drink, and be merry." ' But God said to him, 'You foolish man, this very night your life will be demanded of you, and all this stored-up wealth, what will happen to it then?' Thus will it be with those who store up treasures for themselves on earth, but have no riches waiting for them in heaven."

Passing on to the region of Caesarea Philippi, he asked his disciples, "Who do people say the Son of Man is?" They replied, "Some say John the Baptizer, others say Elijah, still others say Jeremiah or one of the prophets." He said to them, "Who do you say that I am?"

Simon said in reply, "You are the Messiah [the Anointed One], the Son of the Living God." Jesus responded, "Blessed are you, Simon, son of John, because flesh and blood [human reason] has not revealed this to you, but my Father in heaven. So, I say to you, you are Peter [which means "rock"], and on this rock I will build my church, and the gates of hell will never prevail against you. I will give to you the keys of the kingdom of heaven. Whatsoever you shall bind on earth, I will bind in heaven; whatsoever you loose on earth, I will loose in heaven." Then he strictly ordered his disciples to tell no one that he was the Messiah.

Then Jesus began to teach them that the Son of Man would have to suffer many things, that he would be rejected by the elders and the chief priests and the scribes, and be put to death, then, after three days, rise again. He said this to them openly. Peter took Jesus aside and began to admonish him. But turning and noticing his disciples, he scolded Peter, saying to him, "Get behind me, Satan! Because you are not attentive to God's wishes, but your own."

Then Jesus said to his disciples, "Whoever wishes to follow me must deny himself, take up his cross daily, and follow me. For whoever wishes to save his life will lose it, but, whoever loses his life for my sake will save it. What profit is there for someone who gains the whole world but

lose his life? Or what can one give in exchange for his life?
For the Son of Man will come with his angels in his Father's
glory, and then he will repay everyone according to his con-
duct. In truth, I say to you, there are some standing here
who will not taste death until they see the Son of Man
coming in his kingdom."

ELEVEN

S*ix days later*, Jesus took Peter, James, and John, his brother, and led them up a very high mountain by themselves. And he became transfigured before them. His face shone like the sun, his clothes were white like light. And behold, Moses and Elijah appeared to them, conversing with him. Peter said to Jesus, "Lord, it is good for us to be here. If you would like, I will build three booths here, one for you, one for Moses, and one for Elijah." While he was still speaking, a bright cloud cast a shadow over them, and from the cloud came a voice, saying, "This is my beloved Son, with whom I am greatly pleased. Listen to him."

When the disciples heard this, they fell facedown on the

ground, being struck with fear. Jesus came and touched them, saying, "Rise, do not be afraid." When the disciples looked up, they saw no one but Jesus alone.

As they were coming down the mountain, Jesus instructed them, "Tell no one of the vision until the Son of Man has risen from the dead." The disciples then asked him, "Why do the scribes say that Elijah must come first?"

"Elijah will indeed come," Jesus told them, "and restore all things; but I tell you, Elijah has already come, and they did not recognize him, and did whatever they pleased to him. So also will it be with the Son of Man, who will suffer many things at their hands." The disciples realized he was talking about John the baptizer.

Approaching the other apostles, they noticed a crowd surrounding them, and scribes arguing with them. As Jesus approached, the crowd was surprised. They ran up to him and greeted him. "What are you arguing about with them," he asked. Someone from the crowd answered him. "Teacher, I have brought to you my son, who is possessed by a tongue-tied devil. Whenever it seizes him, it throws him down; he foams at the mouth, grinds his teeth, and he becomes rigid. I asked your disciples to drive it out, but they could not do so." He said to them in reply, "O faithless and perverse generation! How long will I have to put up with you? Bring him here to me." They brought the boy to him. And when he saw him, the spirit immediately threw him into convulsions. As he fell to the ground, he began to roll around and foam at the mouth. Then he questioned his father. "How long has this been happening to him?" "Since childhood," he replied. "It has often thrown him into fire and into water to kill him. But if you can do anything, have compassion on us and help us." Jesus said to him, "Everything is possible to one who has faith." The boy's father cried out, "I do believe; help my unbelief." As the crowd of people pressing around him was growing, he reproached the evil spirit. "Deaf and dumb spirit, I command you to come out of him, never to return!" Then the spirit threw him into convulsions and came out of him, shouting. The boy remained lying there like a corpse, causing some of the people to say, "He is dead." Jesus then took him by the hand, lifted him up, and he stood up straight.

When Jesus had entered the house, the disciples asked him, "Why could we not drive it out?" "Because your faith had faltered. This kind," he said, "can come out only by prayer. In truth, I tell you, if you had faith the size of a mustard seed, you could say to this mountain, 'Move yourself from here,' and it would move, or to this mulberry tree, 'Pick yourself up and be planted in the sea' and it would do it. Nothing would be impossible to you."

As the apostles were gathering in Galilee, Jesus said to them, "The Son of Man is to be handed over to men, and they will kill him, and he will be raised up on the third day."

Hearing this, the disciples were overwhelmed with grief. Although they did not understand what he was telling them, as its meaning was hidden from them, they were afraid to ask him.

Entering Capernaum, collectors of the temple tax approached Peter and said, "Doesn't your teacher pay the temple tax?"

"Of course," he said.

When Jesus and the apostles entered the house, and before Simon had a chance to speak, Jesus addressed him: "Simon, what is your opinion? From whom do kings of this world collect tolls and taxes? From their sons or from subjects?" When Simon said, "From subjects," then Jesus said, "So the sons are exempt, then. But to avoid creating an issue, Simon, go down to the sea and cast a line. The first fish you catch will have a coin in its mouth, enough for twice the temple tax. Give it to them for you and for me."

After this the Feast of Tabernacles was near. His brothers said to him, "Leave here and go to Judea, so that your disciples there may see the works you are doing. No one works in secret if he wants to be known publicly. If you do these things, manifest yourself to the world." His brothers themselves did not believe in him.

Jesus said to them, "My time is not yet come, but the time is always right for you. The world cannot hate you, but it hates me, because I testify to them that their works are evil. You go up to the feast. I am not going up to the feast, because my time has not yet been fulfilled." After saying this, he stayed on in Galilee.

When, however, his brothers had gone up to the feast, he himself also went up, not openly, but secretly. The Judeans were looking for him at the feast and saying, "Where is he?" And there was considerable discussion about him among the crowds. Some said, "He is a good man," while others said, "No, on the contrary, he misleads people." Still, no one spoke openly of him for fear of the Judean rulers.

When the feast was already half over, Jesus went up into the temple area and began to teach. The Judeans were shocked, and remarked, "How does he know scripture without having studied?" Jesus answered them, "My teaching is not my own, but is from the One who sent me. Whoever chooses to do His will shall know whether my teaching is from God or whether I speak on my own. Whoever speaks on his own seeks his own glory, but whoever seeks the glory of the One who sent him is truthful, and there is no deceit in him. Did not Moses give you the law? Yet, none of you keeps the law. Why are you trying to kill me?"

The crowd answered, "You are possessed! Who is trying to kill you?"

Jesus answered, "I performed one work and all of you are amazed because of it. Moses gave you circumcision—not that it came from Moses, but from the patriarchs, and you circumcise a man on the sabbath. If a man can be circumcised on the sabbath so that the law of Moses may not be broken, are you angry with me because I made a man well on the sabbath? Stop judging by appearances, but judge with integrity."

Some of the inhabitants of Jerusalem said, "Is he not the one they are trying to kill? And look, he is speaking openly and they say nothing to him. Could it be that the authorities have come to accept him as the Messiah? Yet we know where he comes from. When the Messiah comes, no one will know his origins."

Jesus cried out in the temple area, "You know me and also know whence I came. Yet I did not come on my own, but the One who sent me, whom you do not know, is true. I know Him because I am from Him, and He sent me."

The temple police tried to arrest him, but they dared not lay a hand on him because his hour had not yet come. Many of the crowd, however, began to believe in him, and said, "When the Messiah comes, will he perform more signs than this man has done?"

The Pharisees overheard the people speaking in this way, so the chief priests and Pharisees sent guards to arrest him. So Jesus said, "I will be with you only a little while longer, then I will return to the One who sent me. You will look for me but will not find me, and where I am you cannot come."

The Judean leaders said to one another, "Where is he going that we cannot find him? Surely he is not going to those of the dispersion [Israelites who moved out into other countries], among the Greeks, to teach the Greeks, is he? What is his meaning of the saying 'You will look for me and not find me?' and 'Where I am you cannot come.' "

On the last and greatest day of the feast, Jesus stood up and exclaimed, "Let anyone who thirsts come to me and drink. Whoever believes in me, as scripture says, 'Rivers of living water will flow from within him.' " He said this in reference to the Spirit that those who came to believe in him were to receive. There was, of course, no Spirit yet, because Jesus had not yet been glorified.

Some of the crowd who had heard these words said, "This is truly the prophet." Others said, "This is the Messiah." But others said, "The Messiah will not come from Galilee, will he? Does not the scripture say the Messiah will be of David's family and come from Bethlehem, the village where David lived?" So a division arose among them concerning him. Some of them even wanted to arrest him, but no one laid hands on him.

The guards went to the chief priests and Pharisees, who asked them, "Why did you not bring him?" The guards answered, "Never before has anyone spoke as this man." The Pharisees sneered at them. "Have you also been deceived? Have any of the authorities or the Pharisees believed in him? The crowd who does not know the law is accursed." Nicodemus, one of their members, who had come to Jesus earlier, said to them, "Does our law condemn a person without first hearing him and finding out what he is doing?" They ridiculed him. "You are not from Galilee also, are you? Look and see that no prophet comes from Galilee."

That evening, Jesus' friends went each to his own house, while Jesus went to the Mount of Olives. Early the next morning, he arrived again at the temple area, and a crowd began to gather around him, as he sat down and taught them.

Some scribes and Pharisees brought before him a woman who had been caught in adultery, and made her stand in the middle of the crowd. They said to him, "Rabbi, this woman has been caught in the very act of adultery. Now, in the law, Moses commanded that we stone such a woman. What do you say?" They said this to test him, so they could bring some charge against him. Jesus bent down and began to write in the dust with his finger. But when they continued asking him, he straightened up and said to them, "Let him who is without sin among you cast the first stone." Again he bent down and wrote on the ground. Seeing what he wrote, they went away one by one, beginning with the elders. Then he found himself alone with the woman before him. Straightening, he said to her, "Woman, has no one condemned you?" "No one, sir." Then Jesus said, "Neither will I condemn you. Go and avoid this sin."

Later on, while in the temple precincts, Jesus spoke again, saying, "I am the light of the world. Whoever follows me will have the light of life." The Pharisees accused him,

"You are your own witness, and as such your testimony is unverifiable."

Jesus said, "Even if I testify on my own behalf, my testimony can be verified, because I know where I came from and where I am going. But you do not know where I came from or where I am going. You judge by appearances, but I do not judge anyone. And even if I should judge, my judgment is valid because I am not alone; we are two: I and the Father who sent me. Even in your law it is written that the testimony of two men can be verified. I testify on my behalf and so does the Father who sent me." Then they said, "Where is your father?" Jesus answered, "You know neither me nor my Father. If you knew me, you would know my Father also." He spoke these words while speaking in the treasury in the temple area. No one, however, arrested him, because his hour had not yet come.

He said to them again, "I am going away and you will look for me, but you will die in your sin. Where I am going you cannot come." So the Judeans said, "He is not going to kill himself, is he, because he said, 'Where I am going you cannot come?'" He said to them, "You belong to what is below. I belong to what is above. You belong to this world, but I do not belong to this world. That is why I told you that you will die in your sins. For if you do not believe that I AM, you will surely die in your sins."

They said to him, "Who are you?"

Jesus said to them, "What I told you from the beginning. I have much to say about you in condemnation. But
the One who sent me is truth itself, and what I heard from
Him I tell the world." They did not realize he was speaking
to them of the Father. So Jesus said to them, "When you lift
up the Son of Man, then you will realize that I AM, and that
I do nothing on my own, but say only what the Father
taught me. The One who sent me is with me. He has not left
me alone, because I always do what is pleasing to Him."
Again, because he spoke this way, many believed in him.

Jesus then spoke to those Judean leaders who believed in
him. "If you remain in my word, you will truly be my disciples, and you will come to know the truth, and the truth will
set you free." They replied, "We are descendants of Abraham and have never been enslaved by anyone. How can you
say, 'You will become free?' "

"In truth, I tell you, everyone who commits sin is a slave
of sin. A slave does not remain long in the household, but a
son does. So if a son frees you, then you are free. I know that
you are descendants of Abraham. But your colleagues are
trying to kill me, because my word has no place in their
hearts. I tell you what I have seen in the Father's presence; it
is now for you to do what you have heard from the Father."

They said to him, "Our father is Abraham." Jesus replied, "If you were Abraham's children, you would be doing
the works of Abraham. But now you are trying to kill me, a
man who has told you the truth that he has heard from God.

Abraham did not act like this. You are for sure doing the works of your father." They said to him, "We are not illegitimate. We have only one Father, God."

Jesus said to them, "If God were your Father, you would love me, for I came from God and am here. I did not come on my own; He sent me. Why do you not understand what I am saying? It is because you cannot bear to hear my word. You belong to your father, the devil, and you willingly carry out your father's desires. He was a murderer from the beginning, and does not stand on truth, because there is no truth in him. When he tells a lie, he speaks in character, because he is a liar and the father of lies. But because I speak the truth, you do not believe me. Can any of you charge me with sin? If I am telling the truth, why do you not believe me? Whoever belongs to God hears the words of God. For this reason you do not listen, because you do not belong to God."

The Judeans answered him, "Are we not right in saying that you are a Samaritan and are possessed?" Jesus answered, "I am not possessed. I honor my Father, but you dishonor me. I do not seek my own glory; there is One who seeks it and He is the one who judges.

"In all truth, I say to you, whoever keeps my words will never see death." Then the Judeans said to him, "Now we know for sure that you are possessed; Abraham died, so did the prophets, yet you say, 'Whoever keeps my word will never see death.' Are you greater than Abraham, who died?

101

Or the prophets, who died? Who do you make yourself out to be?"

Jesus answered, "If I glorify myself, my glory is nothing, but it is my Father who glorifies me, of whom you say, 'He is my God.' You do not know Him, but I know Him, and if I should say I do not know Him, I would become like you, a liar. But I do know Him and I keep His word. Abraham your father rejoiced to see my day. He saw it and was glad." So the Judeans said to him, "You are not yet fifty years old, and you have seen Abraham?" Jesus said to them, "In truth, I say to you, before Abraham came to be, I AM" (the Hebrew name for God). They then picked up stones to cast at him, which was the punishment for blaspheming, but Jesus eluded them and left the temple area.

A short distance away, he saw a man blind from birth. His disciples asked him, "Who sinned, this man or his parents, that he should be born blind?" Jesus answered, "Neither he nor his parents sinned. It is that the works of God might be made visible through him. We have to do the works of the One who sent me while it is day. Night is coming, when no one can work. While I am in the world, I am the light of the world." When he had said this, he spat on the ground and made clay with his saliva, and smeared the clay on the man's eyes, and said to him, "Go to the Pool of Siloam [which means "He who is sent"] and wash." So he went and washed, and came back with his sight.

His neighbors and those who had seen him earlier as a

beggar remarked, "Isn't this the one who used to sit and beg?" Some said, "It is," but others said, "No, he just looks like him." He himself said, "I am he." They said to him, "How were your eyes opened?" He replied, "The man called Jesus made clay and anointed my eyes and told me, 'Go to Siloam and wash.' So I went there and washed and was able to see." And they said to him, "Where is he?" He replied, "I don't know."

They brought the one who had been born blind to the Pharisees. Now, Jesus had made clay and opened his eyes on the sabbath. So the Pharisees asked him how he was able to see. He told them, "He put clay on my eyes, and I washed, and now I can see." So some of the Pharisees said, "This man is not from God, because he does not keep the sabbath." But others said, "How can a sinful man do such wonders?" And there was a division among them. So they said to the blind man again, "What do you have to say about him, since he opened your eyes?" He said, "He is a prophet."

Now, these Judeans did not believe that he had been born blind and gained his sight until they summoned the parents of the one who had gained his sight. They asked them, "Is this your son, who you say was born blind? How does he now see?" His parents answered and said, "We know that this is our son and that he was born blind. We do not know how he sees now, nor do we know who opened his eyes. Ask him, he is of age; he can speak for himself." His parents said this because they were afraid of the Judeans, for the Judean rulers had already agreed that if anyone had acknowledged him as the Messiah, he would be expelled from the synagogue. For this reason his parents said, "He is of age; ask him."

So a second time they called the man who had been blind and said to him, "Give God the praise! We know that this man is a sinner." He replied, "Whether he is a sinner or not, I do not know. One thing I do know and that is that I was blind and now I see." So they questioned him, "What did he do to you?" He answered, "I already told you and you did not listen. Why do you want to hear it again? Do you want to become his disciples too?" They ridiculed him and said, "You are that man's disciple; we are disciples of Moses. We know that God spoke to Moses, but this man, we do not know where he comes from." The man replied, "That is surprising that you do not know where he is from, yet he opened my eyes. We know that God does not listen to sinners, but if one is devout and does His will, He listens to him. It is unheard of that anyone ever opened the eyes of a person born blind. If this man were not from God, he would not be able to do anything." They said to him, "You who are steeped in sin dare to teach us." Then they threw him out.

When Jesus heard that they had thrown him out, he found him and said, "Do you believe in the Son of Man?" "Who is he, sir, so that I may believe in him?" Jesus said to him, "You have seen him. The one who is speaking with you is he." "I do believe, Lord." And he fell down and paid Jesus honor.

Jesus then said, "I have come into this world for judgment, so that those who do not see might see, and those who do see will be blind." The Pharisees standing around heard him say this, and immediately challenged him. "Surely you are not saying we are blind?" Jesus said to them, "If you were blind, you would have no sin, but because you say 'We see,' your sins remain."

He then continued. "In truth, I tell you, whoever does not enter the sheepfold through the gate, but climbs over the enclosure, is a thief and a robber. But whoever enters through the gate is the shepherd of the sheep. The gatekeeper opens it for him, and the sheep respond to his voice, as he calls each by name and leads them out. When he has ushered out all his own, he then walks in front of them, and the sheep follow him, because they recognize his voice. But they will not follow a stranger; they will run away from him, because they do not recognize the voice of strangers." Although Jesus used this simile, they did not realize what he was trying to tell them.

So he said again, "Listen to me, I tell you, I am the sheep gate. All who came before me are thieves and bandits, and the sheep do not listen to them. I am the gate. Whoever enters through me will be saved, and will come in and go out and find rich pastureland. A thief comes only to steal and kill and destroy. I came so that they might have life and have it more abundantly. I am the good shepherd. A good shepherd lays down his life for his sheep. A hired hand who is not a shepherd and whose sheep are not his own sees the wolf coming and leaves the sheep and flees. The wolf then comes and catches and scatters the sheep. This is because he is a hired hand and works for pay but has no love for the sheep. I am the good shepherd. I know mine and mine know me, just as the Father knows me and I know the Father, and I will lay down my life for the sheep.

"I have other sheep not of this fold. These also I must lead, and they will hear my voice, and there will be one flock and one shepherd. This is why the Father loves me, because I lay down my life in order to take it up again. No one takes it from me, but I lay it down on my own. I have power to lay it down and I have power to take it up again. This command I have received from my Father."

Again there was a division among the Judeans because of these words. Many of them said, "He is possessed and out of his mind; why listen to him?" Others said, "These are not the words of a madman, or one possessed. Can a demon open the eyes of the blind?"

On another occasion, when Jesus was again in Jerusalem for the Feast of the Dedication, it was during the winter. Jesus walked about in the temple area on the Portico of Solomon. Many Judeans gathered around him and asked, "How long are you going to keep us in suspense? If you are the Messiah, tell us plainly." Jesus answered them, "I told you and you do not believe. The works I do in my Father's name testify to me. But you do not believe, because you are not among my sheep. My sheep hear my voice; I know them and they follow me. I give them eternal life and they shall never perish. No one can take them out of my hand. My father, who has given them to me, is greater than all, and no one can snatch them out of the Father's hand. The Father and I are one."

The Judeans again picked up rocks to stone him. Jesus said to them, "I have shown you many good works from my Father. For which of these do you stone me?" The Judeans answered him, "We are not stoning you for a good work, but for blasphemy. You, a mere man, are making yourself God." Jesus answered them, "Is it not written in your law, 'I said, "You are gods?"' If it calls them gods to whom the word of God came, and scripture cannot lose its force, how can you say that the one whom the Father has consecrated and sent into the world blasphemes because I said, 'I am the Son of God?' If I do not perform my Father's works, do not believe me, but if I perform them, even if you do not believe me, believe the works, so that you may realize and understand that the Father is in me and I am in the Father." They again tried to arrest him, but he eluded them.

While Jesus was wandering through the area outside Judea, a man named Lazarus was ill in Bethany, the village of Martha and Mary. Mary was the one who had anointed the Lord with perfumed oil and dried his feet with her hair.

It was her brother Lazarus who was ill. So the sisters sent word to Jesus, saying, "Master, the one whom you love is ill." When Jesus heard this, he said, "This illness is not fatal; it is for the glory of God, that the Son of God may be glorified through it." Now, Jesus loved Martha and her sister and Lazarus. So when he heard that Lazarus was ill, Jesus remained for two days in the place where he was. Then, after this, he said to his disciples, "Let us go back to Judea." The disciples said to him, "Lord, the Judeans were just trying to stone you, and you want to go back there?"

Jesus answered, "Are there not twelve hours in a day? If one walks during the day, he does not stumble, because he sees the light of the world. But if he walks at night, he stumbles, because the light is not in him." After saying this, he then told them, "Our friend Lazarus is asleep, but I am going to awaken him." The disciples said to him, "Master, if he is asleep, he will be healed." But Jesus was talking about death, though they thought he was talking about a resting sleep. Jesus then told them, "Lazarus is dead. I am glad I was not there, that you might believe. Now let us go to him." Thomas, called Didymus, said to his fellow disciples, "Let us also go to die with him."

When Jesus arrived, he found that Lazarus had already been in the tomb four days. Now, Bethany was near Jerusalem, only about two miles distant. And many of the Judean friends of the family had come to comfort Mary and Martha about their brother. When Martha heard that Jesus was coming, she went out to meet him; but Mary sat at home. Martha said to Jesus, "Lord, if you had been here, my brother would not have died. But even now I know that whatever you ask of God, God will give you." Jesus said to her, "Your brother will rise."

Martha said to him, "I know that he will rise in the resurrection on the last day." Jesus told her, "I am the resurrection and the life. Whoever believes in me, even if he dies, will live. And everyone who lives and believes in me will never die. Do you believe this?" She said to him, "Yes, Lord, I have come to believe that you are the Messiah, the Son of God, the one who is to come into the world."

When she said this, she went and called her sister Mary secretly, saying, "The teacher is here and is asking for you." As soon as she heard this, she rose quickly and went to him. Jesus was not yet in the village, but at the same place where Martha had met him. So when the Judeans who were with her in the house comforting her saw Mary get up quickly and go out, they followed her, presuming she was going to the tomb to weep there. When Mary came to the place where Jesus was, she fell at his feet and said to him, "Lord, if you had been here, my brother would never have died." When Jesus saw her weeping and the Judeans who had come with her weeping, he was deeply moved. He said to her, "Where have you laid him?" They said to him, "Sir, come and see." Then Jesus wept. The Judeans remarked, "See how he loved him!" But some said, "Could not one who opened the eyes of the blind man have done something so this man would not have died?"

Jesus, profoundly moved, arrived at the tomb. It was a cave, and a stone lay across the entrance. Jesus said, "Remove the stone!" Martha, the dead man's sister, said to him, "Lord, by now there will be a stench. He has already been dead for four days." Jesus said to her, "Did I not tell you that if you believe, you will see the glory of God?" So they took away the stone. Jesus raised his eyes and said, "Father, I thank you for hearing me. I know that you always hear me; but because of people here I have said this that they may believe that you sent me." And when he had said this, he shouted out in a loud voice, "Lazarus, come forth!" The dead man came walking out, tied hand and foot with burial bands, and his face was wrapped in a cloth. So Jesus said to them, "Loosen him and let him go."

Many of the Judeans who had come to console Mary and had seen what Jesus had done began to believe in him. But some of them went to the Pharisees and told them what Jesus had done. So the chief priests and the Pharisees convened the Sanhedrin and said, "What are we going to do? This man is performing many signs. If we leave him alone, everyone will believe in him, and the Romans will come and take away everything, our land and our independence." But one of them, Caiaphas, who was high priest of that year, said, "You know nothing. Do you not realize it is better for you that one man should die so the nation may not perish?"

He said this, not on his own, but as high priest for that year he prophesied that Jesus was going to die for the nation, and not only for the nation, but to gather into one the dispersed children of God. So from that day on, they plotted their strategy to kill him. As a result, Jesus no longer walked about in public among the Judeans, but he left for the region near the desert, to a town called Ephraim, and there he remained with his disciples.

Since the feast was over, Jesus returned to Galilee. On the way, the disciples became involved in a heated discussion. When they arrived back at home, Jesus asked them, "What were you arguing about on our way home?" But they remained silent. They had been arguing among themselves as to who was the greatest among them. He then sat down and called the Twelve around him and said to them, "If anyone wishes to be first, he must be last of all, and the servant of all the rest."

On another occasion the disciples approached him and asked, "Lord, who is the greatest in the kingdom of heaven?" He called over a little child, set the child in their midst, and said, "In truth, unless you change and become like this little child, you will not even enter the kingdom of heaven. Whoever humbles himself like this little child is the greatest in the kingdom of heaven. And whoever receives a child such as this in my name receives me. Whoever causes these little ones who believe in me to sin, it would be better for him to have a millstone tied around his neck and he be cast into the sea. See that you do not wound any of these little ones, for I tell you, their angels in heaven forever look on the face of my heavenly Father.

"Woe to the world because of scandals; such things will happen, but woe to the one through whom scandal comes. If your hand or foot is an occasion of sin, cut it off and get rid of it. It is better to enter life crippled and maimed than with two hands and two feet to be cast into eternal fire. And if your eye is an occasion of sin for you, pluck it out and throw it away. It is better to enter into life with one eye than with both eyes to be cast into the fires of Gehenna.

"Be on your guard! If your brother sins, counsel him. If he repents, forgive him. And if he offends you seven times in a day, and comes to you and says 'I am sorry,' forgive him. If he does not accept your counsel, take one or two others along with you, so that one or two witnesses may record every fact. If he refuses to listen to them, tell the church. If he refuses to listen even to the church, then treat him as you would a Gentile or a publican. In truth, I say to you, whatever you bind on earth will be bound in heaven; whatever you loose on earth will be loosed in heaven."

Then Peter approached him and asked, "Lord, if my brother sins against me, how often must I forgive him, seven times?"

Jesus answered, "I tell you, not seven times, but seventy times seven times. That is why the kingdom of heaven can be likened to a king who decided to settle accounts with his servants. When he began the accounting, a debtor was brought in who owed him an enormous amount. As he had no way of paying it, the king ordered him to be sold, together with his wife, his children, and all his property, to satisfy the debt.

"The servant fell down on his knees and did him homage, pleading with him, 'Be patient with me and I will pay you all I owe you.' Moved with compassion, the master of that servant forgave him the whole debt. When, however, that servant left, he found one of his fellow servants who owed him a much smaller amount. He seized him by the throat and almost choked him, demanding, 'Pay me what you owe me.'

"The servant fell on his knees and pleaded, 'Be patient with me and I will pay you all.' But he refused. Instead, he had him thrown into prison until he paid back the debt. Now, when his fellow servants saw what had happened, they were very upset and went to their master and related to him the whole incident. His master then summoned that wicked servant and said to him, 'You miserable wretch, I forgave you your entire debt because you pleaded with me. Should you not have had pity on your fellow servant, as I had pity on you?' Then, in anger, his master turned him over to the torturers until he should pay back his whole debt. So will my heavenly Father do to you if you do not forgive your brother from your heart. Again, I also say to you, if two of you agree on something for which you pray, it will be granted you by my heavenly Father. For where two or three come together in my name, there am I in their midst."

Tax collectors and sinners were all gathering around to listen to him. The Pharisees and scribes began to complain. "This man welcomes sinners, and even eats with them." So he addressed this parable to them. "What man among you having a hundred sheep and losing one of them would not leave the ninety-nine in the fields and go searching for the lost one until he finds it? When he does so, he places it on his shoulders with great joy, and, on arrival back home calls in his friends and neighbors and says to them, 'Celebrate with me. I have found my lost sheep.' I tell you, in just the same way will there be more joy in heaven over one sinner who repents than over ninety-nine righteous who have no need of repentance.

"Or what woman having ten coins, and losing one, would not light a lamp and sweep the house, searching carefully until she finds it? And when she does find it, she calls in her friends and neighbors and says to them, 'Celebrate with me. I have found the coin that I lost.' In just the same way, I tell you, will there be rejoicing among the angels of God over one sinner who repents."

Then he said, "A man had two sons. The younger said to the father, 'Give me the share of the estate that should be mine.' So the father divided the property among them. After a few days, the younger son collected all his belongings and set out for a faraway country, where he squandered his inheritance in loose living. When he had freely spent everything, a severe famine struck that country, and he found himself in desperate need. So, he hired himself out to one of the local citizens, who sent him to his farm to feed pigs. He longed to eat the pods on which the pigs fed, but no one gave him any.

"Coming to his senses, he said to himself, 'How many hired hands on my father's farm have more than enough to eat, while I am here dying of starvation. I shall pack up and go to my father and say to him, "Father, I have sinned against heaven and against you. I no longer deserve to be called your son. Treat me as you would one of your hired hands." ' So he packed up and went back to his father.

"While he was still a long way off, his father caught sight of him and was filled with compassion. He ran to his son, embraced him, and kissed him. His son said to him, 'Father, I have sinned against heaven and against you. I no longer deserve to be called your son.' But his father ordered his servants, 'Quickly bring the finest robe, and put it on him. Put a ring on his finger and sandals on his feet. Take the fattened calf and kill it. Let us celebrate with a feast, because this son of mine was dead and has come to life; he was lost and has been found.' Then the celebration began.

"The older son had been out in the field. On his way back, as he came nearer the house, he heard the sound of music and dancing. Calling one of the servants, he asked what this all meant. The servant said to him, 'Your brother has returned, and your father has slaughtered the fattened calf because he has him back safe and sound.'

"He became angry, and when he refused to enter the house, his father came out and pleaded with him. He said to his father, 'Look, all these years I served you and never once did I disobey your orders. Yet you never gave me even a young goat for me to feast on with my friends. But, when this son of yours returns after having wasted all your possessions on prostitutes, you slaughter the fattened calf.'

"He said to him, 'My son, you are with me always. All that I have is yours. But now we must celebrate and be happy, because your brother was dead and has come to life; he was lost and has been found.'

"Who among you would say to your servant who has just come in working the farm or tending sheep in the field, 'Come right now, and take your place at table.' Would you not rather say, 'Prepare something for me to eat. Put on your apron and wait on me while I eat and drink. When I am finished, then you may eat and drink.' Should he be grateful to that servant for doing the work assigned to him? So it should be with you. When you have done all that has been commanded of you, say, 'We are unprofitable servants; we have done only what we were commanded to do and nothing more.' "

He then said to his disciples (in the hearing of the Pharisees), "A rich man had a steward who was reported to him for squandering his property. He summoned him and said, 'What is this I hear about you? Draw up an account of your stewardship, as you will be steward no longer.'

"The steward said to himself, 'What shall I do now that my master is taking my position away from me? I am not strong enough to dig; I am ashamed to go begging. I know what I shall do, so that, when I am discharged, they will welcome me into their homes.' He called in his master's debtors one by one. To the first he said, 'How much do you owe my master?' 'One hundred measures of olive oil' was his reply. 'Here is your bond, sit down right now and write fifty,' he said. To another debtor he said, 'And you, how much do you owe?' He replied, 'One hundred measures of wheat.' 'Here is your bond, write down eighty.' Now the master commended the dishonest steward for acting shrewdly. The children of this world are much shrewder in dealing with their own kind than are the children of the light. I tell you, make friends for yourselves with ill-gotten wealth, so when it is spent, your dishonest partners can then give you a warm welcome into heaven. Whoever is trustworthy in small matters can be trusted as well in important ones; whoever is dishonest in small matters will also be dishonest in important affairs. If, therefore, you are not trustworthy with ill-gained wealth, how can you be trusted with honest wealth? If you are not trustworthy with what belongs to another, who will even feel safe giving you what is rightfully yours? No servant can serve two masters. Either he will hate one and love the other, or he will be devoted to one and despise the others. You cannot serve God and money."

The Pharisees, who loved money, heard all these things and ridiculed him. He said to them, "You justify yourselves in the sight of others, but God knows your hearts. What is valuable to humans is worthless to God. The law and the prophets continued right up till John's coming. From then the kingdom of God [founded on love] was proclaimed, and people rushed in force to enter. But the law will last until all is fulfilled, for it is easier to imagine heaven and earth passing away than for God's law to lose its force."

One day, John came up to Jesus and said to him, "Master, we saw someone driving out devils in your name, and we tried to prevent him because he is not one of our company." Jesus replied, "Do not prevent him. No one who does an outstanding work in my name can be against me. And, whoever is not against us is for us. Anyone who gives you a cup of water because you belong to the Messiah, I assure you, will not lose his reward."

TWELVE

As *Jesus was aware* the time was approaching for him to be taken up, he resolutely set his face toward Jerusalem. On the way they were to pass through Samaria, then east of the Jordan, and back through Jericho into Judea. Before beginning the journey, however, the Lord appointed seventy-two others whom he sent ahead, two by two, to every town and place he intended to visit. He told them, "The harvest is abundant, but the laborers are few. Ask the master of the harvest to send out laborers for his harvest. Go on your way, and note well, I am sending you like lambs among wolves, so be as sly as a fox but as innocent as a dove. Carry no moneybag, no sack, no sandals, and greet no one along the way. Into whatever house you enter, first say, 'Peace to this house.' If there are peaceable people who live there, your peace will rest on them, but if not, it will return to you. Stay in the same house and eat and drink what they offer you, for the laborer deserves his wages. Do not move from house to house. Whatever town you enter and they welcome you, eat what is set before you, cure the sick there, and say to them, 'The kingdom of God has come to this house.' Whatever town you enter and they do not receive you, go out into the streets and say, 'The very dust of your streets that clings to our feet we kick off as witness against you.' I tell you, the kingdom of God is fast approaching, and it will go easier for Sodom on that day than for that town."

Then he began to lament those towns where he worked most of his miracles, because they refused to turn from their evil ways. "Woe to you, Chorazin! Woe to you, Bethsaida! If the miracles worked in you had been performed in Tyre and Sidon [pagan towns], they would have long since humbled themselves in sackcloth and ashes. I tell you, it will be more bearable for Tyre and Sidon in the Day of Judgment than for you. And you, Capernaum, did you not aspire for greatness? I tell you, you will be cast down to the lowest pit of hell, for if the miracles done in you had been performed in Sodom [an evil city destroyed in a rain of molten rock], it would still be standing. I tell you, it will still be more bearable for Sodom on the Day of Judgment than for you.

"Whoever listens to you, listens to me. Whoever rejects you, rejects me. And whoever rejects me, rejects the One who sent me."

Later on, the seventy-two returned all excited. "Lord," they said, "even the demons are subject to us because of your name."

Jesus said, "I have observed Satan fall like lightning from the sky. Take heed, I have given you power to tread upon serpents and scorpions, and all the powers of hell, and nothing will harm you. But, rejoice not because spirits are subject to you, but because your names are written in heaven."

A short time later, however, they entered a certain Samaritan town to announce his coming there. The townsfolk refused to welcome him because he was on his way to Judea and Jerusalem. (Judeans and Samaritans had been feuding for centuries, ever since the Samaritans were excommunicated by the Jewish religious leaders for marrying soldiers of an invading pagan army, thus contaminating their Hebrew blood.)

Witnessing this rejection, James and John asked Jesus, "Lord, should we call down fire from heaven to consume them?" Jesus turned and upbraided them, calling them the "sons of thunder" because of their violent tempers, then they left for another village. On their way, a scribe approached him and said, "I will follow you wherever you go." Jesus responded, "Foxes have their dens, the birds of the air have their nests, but the Son of Man has nowhere to even lay his head."

To another he said, "Come, follow me!" But the man replied, "Let me first go and bury my father." Jesus answered him, "Let the dead, and those who will not follow us, bury the dead, but you, go and proclaim the kingdom of God." And another said to him, "I will follow you, Lord, but let me first go home and bid farewell to my family." Jesus responded, "No one who sets his hand to the plow and looks back longingly on what he has left behind is ready for the kingdom of God."

An expert in the law came up to Jesus to test him. "What must I do to possess eternal life?" he asked. "What is written in the law?" Jesus responded, "How do you read it?" The lawyer replied, "You shall love the Lord your God with your whole heart, with your whole soul, with your whole mind, and with all your strength, and your neighbor as yourself." "You have answered rightly," Jesus said. "Do this and you will have life."

Wishing, however, to justify himself, he said to Jesus, "But who is my neighbor?" Jesus replied, "A man was going down from Jerusalem to Jericho and he encountered a band of hoodlums. They robbed him and beat him and left him lying there half dead. A priest happened to be going down that road. He saw the man lying there, and walking to the other side of the road, passed him by. Shortly after, a Levite [a temple attendant] was passing the spot, and seeing the man lying there, crossed to the other side of the road and passed him by. Then a Samaritan man, traveling by, came upon him and, moved with compassion at the sight, walked over to the man, poured oil and wine on his wounds, then bandaged them. Lifting the man up, he placed him on his own mount, took him to an inn, and cared for him. The next day, he took out two silver coins and gave them to the innkeeper with the instructions, 'Take care of him, and I, on my return journey, will pay you what I owe you.' Which of these three, in your opinion, showed himself neighbor to that poor wretch?"

The lawyer answered, "The one who had pity on him." Jesus said to him, "Go and do likewise."

Entering Judea, he passed through a village where he was met by ten lepers. They stood at a distance from him and shouted, "Jesus, Lord, have pity on us!" When he saw them, he said to them, "Go, show yourselves to the priests." As they were on their way, they were cleansed. One of them, realizing he had been healed, returned, glorifying God in a loud voice, then, falling at Jesus' feet, he thanked him. And he was a Samaritan. Jesus said to him, "Were not ten made clean? Where are the other nine? Has no one returned to give thanks to God but this stranger?" Then he said to him, "Stand up and be on your way; your faith has saved you."

A group of Pharisees came up to him and asked him when the kingdom of God would come. He said to them, "The coming of the kingdom of God cannot be seen by human eyes, and no one will announce, 'Look, here it is,' or 'There it is.' For, I tell you, the kingdom of God is already here."

Then he said to his disciples, "The days are coming when you will long to see just one day of the Son of Man, but you will not see it. There will be those who will say to you, 'Look, there he is' or 'Look, here he is.' Do not run off looking for him. For just as lightning flashes across the sky, lighting up the heavens, so will be the coming of the Son of Man when his time comes. But first he must suffer much and be rejected by this generation. As it was in the days of Noah, so it will be in the days of the Son of Man; they were eating and drinking, marrying and giving in marriage right up to the day when Noah entered the ark, and the flood came and destroyed them all. Similarly, as it was in the days of Lot; they were eating and drinking, buying and selling, planting and building; and on the day when Lot left Sodom, fire and molten rock rained down from the sky and destroyed them all. So it will be on the day when the Son of Man is revealed.

"When that day comes, whoever is on their rooftop must not go back to the house to retrieve their belongings, and whoever is in the fields must not go back to what is left behind. Remember the wife of Lot. Whoever seeks to save his life will lose it; and whoever loses his life will save it. I tell you, on that night there will be two people in bed; one will be taken and the other left. And there will be two women grinding grain together; one will be taken, the other left."

They then asked him, "Lord, where will this happen?" "Where the vultures gather, there you will find the carcass," he replied.

Then he told them a parable about the necessity of praying always and not becoming discouraged. "There was a judge in a certain town," he said, "who feared neither God nor human beings. A widow in that town came to him and said, 'I want justice against my adversary.' For a long time, the judge refused to listen to her, but eventually he said to himself, 'Though I fear neither God nor man, if I don't give this woman justice, she will wear me out, and perhaps even do me harm.' Now listen to what this corrupt judge decided. Will not God see that justice is done to His chosen ones when they plead with Him day and night, even though He may at times seem slow to answer? I assure you He will make certain that justice is done, and quickly. But do you think the Son of Man will find faith upon the earth when he comes?"

Jesus then addressed this parable to those who considered themselves righteous and despised everyone else. "Two men went up to the temple to pray. One was a Pharisee, the other a tax collector. The Pharisee walked up through the sanctuary and with arms outstretched prayed thus: 'I thank you, God, that I am not like the rest of men, thieves, extortioners, adulterers, or like that tax collector back there. I fast twice a week. I give one tenth of my income to support the temple. I give alms to the poor.'

"In the back of the temple stood the tax collector, with head bowed, and beating his breast, as he prayed, 'God, be merciful, for I am a sinner.'

"I tell you, that man went home justified in the eyes of God, whereas the other left without God's favor. Everyone who exalts himself will be humbled, and everyone who humbles himself will be exalted."

As he was approaching Jericho, a blind man was sitting by the side of the road, begging. His name was Bar-Timaeus. Hearing a crowd going by, he asked what was happening. They told him Jesus of Nazareth was passing through. He shouted, "Jesus, Son of David, have pity on me!" The people nearby tried to silence him, but he yelled out all the more, "Son of David, have pity on me!"

Jesus stopped and directed that the man be brought to him. When he came near, Jesus asked him, "What is it you would like me to do for you?" "Lord, that I may see." "Receive your sight. Your faith has saved you." He immediately received his sight, and began to follow him, giving glory to God. When the people witnessed this, they also gave praise to God.

At this time the Passover was near, and many went up to Jerusalem beforehand to purify themselves. They looked for Jesus and said to one another as they wandered in the temple area, "What do you think? Will he come to the feast?" For the chief priests and the Pharisees had given orders that if anyone knew his whereabouts, he should inform them, so they might arrest him.

Pharisees in the crowd came up to him and asked, "Is it lawful for a husband to divorce his wife?" In asking this they were setting a trap. In reply, Jesus asked them, "What did Moses say?" "Moses allowed him to write a bill of divorce, then dismiss her," they replied. Jesus told them, "It was because of the hardness of your hearts that Moses wrote you this commandment. It was not so in the beginning, when 'God created them male and female. And for this reason, a man shall leave his father and mother, and hold fast to his wife, so the two become one flesh. Therefore, what God has joined together, no human being may ever separate.' "

In the house, where they were visiting friends, the disciples questioned him, and he said to them, "Whoever divorces his wife and marries another commits adultery against her, and if she divorces her husband and marries another, she commits adultery."

Later, people were bringing their children to Jesus to have him touch them. The disciples, however, were shocked and tried to send them away. When Jesus saw this, he became angry with them, and said to them, "Leave the children alone, let them come to me, for the kingdom of God belongs to such as these. In truth, I tell you, whoever does not accept the kingdom of God like a little child will not enter it." Then he embraced them and, placing his hands on them, blessed them.

As Jesus was walking along, a man ran up to him, knelt down before him, and asked him, "Good teacher, what must I do to gain eternal life?" Jesus asked him, "Why do you call me good? God alone is good. You know the commandments: 'You shall not kill. You shall not commit adultery. You shall not steal. You shall not bear false witness. You shall not defraud. Honor your father and mother.' "

"Teacher, all these things I have done from my youth."

Jesus looked at him with love, and said to him, "If you would be perfect, go sell what you have, give to the poor, and your treasure will be in heaven, then, come follow me." With that, the man's face fell, and he walked away sad, for he had many possessions.

Jesus looked around at his disciples and said to them, "How difficult it is for a rich person to enter the kingdom of God." The disciples were shocked at his words. So Jesus said to them, "Children, how hard it is to enter the kingdom of God. It is easier for a camel to pass through the eye of a needle than for a rich person to enter the kingdom of God." The disciples were even more shocked at his emphasizing his point, and discussed among themselves, "Who, then, can be saved?" Jesus looked at them and said, "For human beings it is impossible, but for God all things are possible."

Peter then said to him, "We have given up everything to

follow you." Jesus responded, "In truth, I tell you, there is no one who has given up house, or brothers or sisters or mother or father, or children or lands for my sake and for the sake of the gospel, who will not be repaid a hundred times over in houses, brothers, sisters, mothers, children, lands, in this life, and persecution as well, and in the age to come, eternal life. But those who pride themselves on being first will find themselves overlooked, and those willing to take the last place will find themselves ahead of the others."

As he entered Jericho, intending just to pass through, an incident occurred. There lived in the village a man named Zacchaeus. He was the chief tax collector and a very wealthy man. Having heard of Jesus, he wanted very much to see him, but being short in stature, he was unable to do so, as a crowd hid Jesus from view. He ran ahead and climbed a sycamore tree overlooking the street, so he could get a glimpse of Jesus as he passed by.

Reaching the place, Jesus stopped, looked up into the tree, and said to him, "Zacchaeus, come down quickly, for today I must stay at your house." He came down quickly and welcomed Jesus with joy. When the people saw this, they complained, "He is going to stay at the house of a sinner?" But Zacchaeus stood his ground and said to Jesus, "Lord, I tell you now, I am giving half of all my possessions to the poor, and if I have extorted anyone, I will return it four fold."

Jesus then said, "This day salvation has come to this

house, because this man, too, is a son of Abraham. The Son of Man has come to seek and save what was lost."

Continuing on their way up to Jerusalem, Jesus was walking ahead of the others. They were surprised, as he had mentioned that he would have to undergo persecution there. The disciples were walking slowly, delaying as much as they could, as they were afraid of what lay ahead. Taking the Twelve aside, Jesus began to tell them what was about to happen. "When we arrive at Jerusalem, the Son of Man will be handed over to the chief priests and the scribes; they will condemn him to death, then turn him over to the Gentiles, who will mock him and spit upon him, then scourge him, and put him to death. But in three days he will arise."

While they were listening to him speak, he proceeded to tell them a parable because he was near Jerusalem, and they thought that the kingdom of God would appear there at any moment. He said, "A man of noble birth went off to a distant country to obtain the kingship that was rightfully his, and then return. He summoned ten of his servants and gave them ten gold coins, and told them, 'Invest these until I return.'

"His fellow citizens, however, hated him, and sent a delegation with the message 'We do not want this man as king over us.' When he returned, after obtaining the kingship, he had those servants to whom he had given the money summoned before him to report on their investments.

"The first came forward and said, 'Sir, your gold coin

has earned ten more.' 'Well done, good servant. You have been faithful in a small matter; now take command of ten cities.' The second came forward and reported, 'Sir, your gold coin has earned five more.' 'Well done, faithful servant. You have been faithful in a small matter; now take command of five cities.' The next one came forward and said, 'Sir, here is your gold coin. I know you are a hard man, and you take up what you did not lay down, and you reap what you did not sow.'

" 'With your own words I will condemn you, you wicked servant. You knew I was a hard person, taking up what I did not lay down, and reaping what I did not sow. Why, then, did you not put my money in a bank so it could have at least drawn interest?' To those standing by he said, 'Take the gold coin from him and give it to him who has ten.' 'Sir, he already has ten coins,' they said to him. 'I tell you,' he said, 'to everyone who has more will be given, but from the one who has not, even that which he has will be taken away. Now, as for my enemies who did not want me as king, bring them here and execute them in my presence.' "

Jesus told another parable on the danger of loving riches. "There was a rich man who dressed in purple garments and fancy linen. He also had sumptuous parties almost daily. Lying at the gate of his mansion was a poor man, named Lazarus, covered with sores, who craved to have just some of the leftovers that fell from the rich man's table. Moreover, dogs used to come and lick the poor man's sores.

When the poor man died, angels came and carried him to heaven, where Abraham himself welcomed him with a warm embrace. The rich man also died and was buried, and from the depths of Gehenna, where he was in torment, he looked up and saw Abraham far away and Lazarus at his side. And he cried out to him, 'Father Abraham, have pity on me. Send Lazarus to dip the tip of his finger in water and cool my tongue, for I am burning up in this torment.'

"Abraham replied, 'My child, remember that you received good things in your life, while Lazarus received nothing but misery. Now he is comforted here, and you are in torment. Moreover, there is a great void between you and us, which prevents anyone from crossing over from our place to yours or from yours to ours.'

"He said, 'Then, I beg you, father, send him to my father's house, for I have five brothers, so he may warn them lest they, too, end up in this place of torment.'

"But Abraham replied, 'They have Moses and the prophets. Let them listen to them.' He said, 'No, father Abraham, but if someone were to go back to them from the dead, they would surely listen and repent.' Then Abraham said, 'If they will not listen to Moses and the prophets, neither will they listen even if someone comes back to them from the dead.' "

THIRTEEN

Jesus then proceeded up to Jerusalem. As he drew near Bethphage and Bethany at the place called the Mount of Olives, he told two of his disciples, "Go into the village opposite you, and as you enter it you will find a colt tethered which no one has ever ridden. Untie it and bring it here. If anyone should ask 'What are you doing, untying that colt?' answer, 'The Master has need of it.' "

So those who had been sent went off and found everything just as he had told them. As they were untying the colt, its owners said to them, "Why are you untying the colt?" They answered, "The Master has need of it." So they brought it to Jesus, threw their cloaks over the colt, and helped Jesus to mount. As he rode along, people were spreading their cloaks along the road. As he approached the slope of the Mount of Olives, the whole multitude of his followers began to praise God aloud with joy for all the mighty deeds they had seen. They proclaimed, "Blessed is he who comes in the name of the Lord.

"Peace in heaven and glory in the highest."

Some of the Pharisees in the crowd said to him, "Teacher, rebuke your disciples."

He said in reply, "I tell you, if they keep silent, the stones themselves will cry out."

Reaching the crest of the mount, he saw the city and wept over it, saying, "If this day you only knew what will bring you peace, but now it is hidden from your eyes. For the days are coming when your enemies will raise a rampart against you and hem you in on every side. They will beat you to the ground and your children within you, and they will not leave in you one stone upon another because you have not known the time of your visitation."

Crossing the valley, he went up into the city and entered the temple area and looked around. As it was late, he and the disciples left and went out to Bethany with the Twelve.

The next day, as they were leaving Bethany, Jesus was hungry. Seeing from a distance a fig tree in leaf, he went over to pick figs from it. When he reached the tree, he found nothing on it but leaves; it was not the time for figs.

And he said to the tree, "May no one ever eat of your fruit again." And his disciples heard it.

Entering Jerusalem, he approached the temple area and saw people buying and selling animals for the sacrifice. Taking a rope, he tied it into knots and proceeded to drive out those doing business. He overturned the tables of the moneychangers and the seats of those who were selling doves. "Take these out of here," he said to them; "is it not written 'My house shall be called a house of prayer for all peoples, but you have turned it into a den of thieves.'" He would not allow anyone to carry anything through the temple area.

His disciples recalled the words of scripture, "Zeal for your house will consume me." The rulers came up to Jesus and demanded, "What sign can you give us authorizing you to do this?" He said to them, "Destroy this temple and in three days I will raise it up." They responded, "This temple took forty-six years to build and you will raise it up in three days?" But he was speaking about the temple of his body. And when he was raised from the dead, his disciples remembered these words, and they believed the scripture and the words he had spoken.

While he was in Jerusalem for the Feast of Passover, many began to believe in his name when they saw the signs he was doing. However, he would not trust himself to them because he knew them all, and did not need anyone to teach him about human nature, as he himself understood it well.

The chief priests and the scribes heard of what he had done, and were seeking a way to put him to death, but they were afraid of him, as the whole crowd venerated him because of his teaching. As evening approached, Jesus and his disciples left the city.

Early the next morning, as they were walking along, the disciples saw that the fig tree had withered to its roots. Peter remembered and said to him, "Rabbi, look! The fig tree that you cursed has withered." Jesus said to them in reply, "Have faith in God. In truth, I tell you, if you have faith, there is nothing that is not possible. Whatever you ask for in prayer, believe that you will receive it and it will be yours. When you stand to pray, forgive whoever has offended you, so that your heavenly Father may forgive you your offenses."

They continued on to Jerusalem, and were walking in the temple area, when the chief priests, the scribes, and the elders came up to Jesus and questioned him. "By what authority do you do the things you do? Who gave you the authority to do them?"

Jesus said to them, "I will ask you one question. Answer for me that one question, and I will tell you by what authority I do the things I do. Was John's baptism of divine or human origin? Answer that for me." They discussed it among themselves, and thought, "If we say, 'Of divine origin,' he will say, 'Why, then, did you not believe him?' If we say, 'Of human origin,' we have reason to fear the crowd, for they regard John as a prophet." So they said to Jesus, "We do not know."

"Neither will I tell you by what authority I do the things I do," Jesus responded to them. Then he began speaking to them in parables. "A man planted a vineyard, put a hedge around it, dug a wine press, built a tower. Then he leased it to tenant farmers, and left on a journey. In due time, he sent a servant to pick up some of the produce of the vineyard. But they seized him, beat him, and sent him away with nothing. The owner then sent another servant. That one they beat over the head and treated him disgracefully. He sent still another, whom they actually killed. So, also, a number of others, some of whom they beat, others they killed. He had one other whom he could send, his beloved son. He finally decided to send him, thinking, 'They will certainly respect my son.'

"But the tenants said to one another, 'This is the heir. Let us kill him, and the inheritance will be ours.' So they seized him, killed him, then threw his body outside the vineyard. What will the owner of the vineyard do? He will come, have the tenants executed, then turn the vineyard over to others. I am sure you have read the scripture passage, 'The stone which the builders rejected has become the cornerstone. By the Lord this has been done, and it is marvelous to see with our own eyes.'"

Knowing the parable was directed at them, they wished

they could have arrested him, but were afraid of the crowd. So they turned and walked away.

After they left, they sent some Pharisees and Herodians to trap him in his speech. (Herodians were loyal to the pagan king, and the Pharisees would ordinarily not socialize with them. But in their hatred of Jesus, they now had a common cause.) They came to him and asked him, "Teacher, we know you are a truthful man, and care little for human respect, but teach what is right regardless of people's reaction. Tell us, is it lawful to pay tribute to Caesar? Should we pay the taxes or not?"

Knowing their hypocrisy, he said to them, "Why do you try to trap me? Show me the coin used to pay the tax." They brought him one. "Whose image and inscription is engraved on it?" he asked them. They replied to him, "Caesar's."

So Jesus said to them, "Repay, then, to Caesar what belongs to Caesar, and to God the things that are God's." They were stunned at his answer.

Then some Sadducees, wealthy Judean rulers who adopted Greek philosophy and did not believe in life after death, came to him. They posed to him this question: "Teacher, Moses wrote for us, 'If someone's brother dies, leaving his wife but no children, his brother must take the wife and raise up descendants for his brother.' Now, there were seven brothers. The first married the woman and died, leaving no descendants. Then the second married her and died, without issue, and the third likewise. The seventh finally married her and had no children by her. Last of all, the woman died. At the resurrection, when they all come back to life, whose wife will she be, for all seven were married to her?"

Jesus said to them, "You have missed the mark, since you know neither the scriptures nor the power of God. When they rise from the dead, they neither marry nor are given in marriage, but are like the angels in heaven. As for the dead being raised, have you not read in the book of Moses, in the passage about the burning bush, how God told him, 'I am the God of Abraham, and the God of Isaac, and the God of Jacob?' He is not God of the dead, but of the living. See how greatly misled you are?"

One of the scribes standing nearby and hearing how well Jesus had answered the Sadducees came up and asked him, "Which is the first of all the commandments?" Jesus replied, "The first is this, 'Hear, O Israel! The Lord our God is Lord alone. You shall love the Lord your God with all your mind, with all your heart, with all your soul, and with all your strength.' The second is like it. 'You shall love your neighbor as yourself.' There is no other commandment that is greater than these."

The scribe said, "Well said, teacher. You are right in saying, 'He is the One, and there is no other than He, and to love Him with all your heart, with all your understanding, with all your strength, and to love your neighbor as yourself is worth more than all the burnt offerings and sacrifices.' "

When Jesus saw that he had an open mind, he said to him, "You are not far from the kingdom of God." From that moment, no one dared to ask him any more questions.

While Jesus was teaching in the temple area, he made the remark, "How do the scribes claim that the Messiah is David's son? David himself, inspired by the Holy Spirit, said, 'The Lord said to my Lord, "Sit at my right hand until I place your enemies under your feet."' David calls him Lord, so how could he be his son?" The crowd listened to the remark with glee, as there were scribes in the audience.

Jesus continued. "Beware of the scribes, who like to strut around in flowing robes, and are fond of greetings in the marketplaces, seats of honor in synagogues, and places of honor at banquets, while secretly they devour the houses of widows, and as a cover-up, recite lengthy prayers. They will receive a bitter judgment."

When he finished speaking, he sat down opposite the treasury and observed how the crowd put money into the treasury. Many rich people put in large sums. A poor widow came along and put in two small coins worth about a penny. Bringing it to his disciples' attention, he remarked, "In truth, I tell you, this poor widow has put in more than all the others, for they gave of their leftovers, but she, from her need, gave all she had, her livelihood."

While Jesus and his disciples were making their way out of the temple, one of his disciples said to him, "Look, teacher, how beautifully the building gleams in the sun, how marvelous is the construction." Jesus said to him, "Do you see these magnificent buildings? One day there will not be left one stone upon another. It will all be thrown down."

Walking across the Kedron Valley, and up the Mount of Olives, opposite the temple area, they sat down to rest. Peter, James, John, and Andrew asked him privately, "Tell us, when will this happen, and what will be the signs that all these things are coming to an end?" Jesus said to them, "Do not let anyone deceive you. Many will come in my name, saying, 'I am he,' and they will deceive many. When you hear of wars and reports of wars, do not be alarmed; these things happen, but it will not be the end. Nation will rise up against nation, and kingdom against kingdom. There will be earthquakes in various places, and there will be famines. These are the beginnings of the labor pains.

"When you see the ultimate abomination standing where he should not be, then those in Judea must flee to the mountains. Woe to pregnant women and nursing mothers in those days! Pray that this does not happen in winter. For those times will have tribulation such as has not been seen since the beginning of creation until now, will ever be seen again. If the Lord had not shortened those days, no one would be saved, but for the sake of the elect whom he chose, those days will be shortened. Be watchful, I have told it all to you beforehand.

"But in those days after the tribulation, the sun will be darkened, the moon will not give its light, the stars will fall from the skies, and the stability of the heavens will be shaken. Then they will see the Son of Man coming in the clouds with great power and majesty. He will send out his angels to gather the elect from the four winds, from the end of the earth to the end of the sky.

"Learn a lesson from the fig tree. When its branch becomes tender and sprouts leaves, you know that summer is near. In the same way, when you see these things happening, know that he is near, at the very gates. In truth, I tell you, this generation will not pass away before these things come to pass. Heaven and earth may pass away but my words will not pass away.

"But of that day or hour, no one knows, neither the angels in heaven, nor the Son, but only the Father. Be on the watch, therefore, and be alert, for you never know when that time will come. Do not let your hearts become lazy with careless living, or become preoccupied with the anxieties of life, or that day will catch you unprepared like a trap. It will be like a man who travels abroad. He leaves home and places his servants in charge, each with his responsibilities, and orders the gatekeeper to be on guard. Be on guard, therefore; you do not know when the lord of the house will return, whether in the evening, or at midnight, or at cockcrow, or in the morning. May he not come suddenly and find you asleep. My word of warning to you and to everyone is 'Keep your eyes open.' "

During the day, Jesus taught in the temple area. At night, however, he would leave and stay at the place called the Mount of Olives. People would rise early in the morning and go out to listen to him.

FOURTEEN

The Passover and the Feast of Tabernacles were to be celebrated in two days. This was the time when the people would commemorate their forty-year sojourn in the desert after leaving Egypt. Every year they would sleep in tents on the hills outside Jerusalem. The chief priests and scribes were trying to find an underhanded way to arrest Jesus and put him to death. They said, however, "Not during the festival, or there may be a riot among the people."

At this time, Jesus was staying with Mary, Martha, and Lazarus at their home in Bethany, only a short distance from Jerusalem. At dinner one day, as they were reclining at table, a woman came up to Jesus with an alabaster jar of perfumed oil, an expensive spikenard. She broke open the alabaster vessel and poured the oil on Jesus' head. Some of those sitting around were offended. Judas was one of them, and he remarked, "What a waste! Why wasn't this sold for three hundred days' wages and the money given to the poor?" But he said this, however, not because he was concerned for the poor, but because he was a thief. He held the common purse for Jesus and the apostles, and he used to steal money for himself. Some others were angry because the woman did this.

Jesus, noticing how they were criticizing the woman, said, "Leave her alone! Why do you try to shame her? She has done a good deed for me. You have the poor with you always, and whenever you wish you can do good to them, but you will not always have me. She has done what she could, and in doing this she is preparing my body for burial.

"In truth, I tell you, wherever the good news is proclaimed throughout the whole world, what she has done will be told in her memory."

Shortly afterward, Judas Iscariot, one of the Twelve, went to the chief priests offering to hand Jesus over to them. When they heard him, they were delighted and promised to pay him money. From then on, he looked for an opportunity to deliver him into their hands.

On the first day of the Feast of Unleavened Bread, when they sacrificed the Passover lamb, Jesus' disciples asked him, "Where do you want us to go and prepare for you to eat the

Passover?" He then sent two of his disciples and told them, "Go into the city and a man carrying a jar of water will meet you. Follow him. Wherever he enters, say to the master of the house, 'The teacher says, "Where is my guest room where I may eat the Passover with my disciples?" ' Then he will show you a large upper room furnished and ready. Make the preparations for us there."

The disciples went off and found it just as he had told them; and they prepared the Passover.

As the Feast of Passover was about to begin, Jesus knew that the hour had come for him to pass from this world to the Father. He had loved those whom his Father had given him in this world, and would love them to the end. The devil had already led Judas, the Iscariot, to betray Jesus, so during the supper, fully aware that the Father had put everything into his power, and that he had come from God and was about to return to Him, he rose from the supper table, took off his cloak, and wrapped a towel around his waist. He then poured water into a basin, and began to wash the feet of his disciples, and dry them with the towel. When he came to Simon Peter, Simon said to him, "Master, you are going to wash my feet?" Jesus answered, "Right now, Peter, you do not understand, but one day you will." "Never," Peter protested, "you will never wash my feet." Jesus replied, "If I do not wash you, then you can have no part with me." "Well, Lord, if it means that much," Simon Peter replied, "then don't just wash my feet, but my hands and head as well." Jesus said, "No one who has bathed needs to be washed. He is clean all over. You, too, are clean, but not all of you are clean." He knew who was going to betray him, that is why he said, "though not all of you."

When he had washed their feet and put his cloak back on, he again reclined at table. He then said to them, "Do you realize what I have just done for you? You call me Lord, and rightly so, for so indeed I am. But if I who am your Lord and Master can get on my knees and wash your feet, so you should do for one another. I have given you a model to follow, so that, just as I have done, you also should do. Listen, I tell you, no slave is greater than his master, nor is any messenger greater than the one who sent him. If you understand this, you will be truly happy if you act on it. I am not speaking about all of you. I know those whom I have chosen. But that the scripture might be fulfilled, 'One who eats at my table with me has turned against me.' I tell you this before it happens, so that when it does happen, you may believe that I AM who I say I am. I assure you, whoever welcomes the one I send welcomes me, and whoever welcomes me welcomes him who sent me."

Having said this, Jesus became deeply troubled and announced for all to hear, "Listen to me, for I tell you, one of you will betray me." The apostles looked at one another in bewilderment, wondering whom he meant. The disciple Jesus loved was reclining next to Jesus. Simon Peter signaled to him to ask Jesus who he means. Leaning back on

Jesus' breast, he asked, "Who is it, Lord?" "It is the one to whom I give the piece of bread that I shall dip in the sauce." He dipped the piece of bread and gave it to Judas, son of Simon Iscariot. At that moment, after taking the bread, Satan entered into him. Jesus then said to him, "What you are about to do, do quickly!" None of the others at table understood the reason he said this. Since Judas had charge of the common fund, some of them thought that Jesus was telling him, "Buy what we need for the festival," or go out and give something to the poor. As soon as Judas had taken the piece of bread, he went out. And the darkness of night had fallen.

When he had gone, Jesus said, "Now has the Son of Man been glorified, and in him God has been glorified. If God has been glorified in him, God will in turn glorify him in himself, and will glorify him very shortly. My children, I will be with you only a little while longer. You will look for me, and as I have told the Judeans, 'Where I go you cannot come,' so now I say it to you.

"I now give you a new commandment: Love one another. As I have loved you, so also should you have love for one another. This is how all will know that you are my disciples, if you have love for one another."

Simon Peter said to him, "Lord, where are you going?"

Jesus answered him, "Where I am going you cannot come now, though you will follow me later." Peter continued. "Lord, why cannot I follow you now? I will lay down my life for you."

Jesus answered, "Will you indeed lay down your life for me? I tell you, before the cock crows, Simon, you will have denied me three times."

FIFTEEN

"*Do not let* your hearts be troubled. You trust in God, trust in me as well. In my Father's house there are many places to live and wander. If it were not so, would I have told you I was going to prepare a place for you? And if I go to prepare a place for you, I will come back and take you with me, so that where I am you also may be. And where I am going you even know the way."

Thomas said to him, "Lord, we do not know where you are going. How could we possibly know the way?"

Jesus told him, "I am the way, the truth, and the life. No one comes to the Father except through me. If you know me, then you also know the Father. As of now you already know the Father, and you have seen Him."

Philip said to him, "Lord, let us see the Father and we will understand."

Jesus said to him, "Have you been with me all this time, and you still do not know me? Philip, whoever sees me sees the Father. How can you say, 'Let us see the Father?' Do you not believe I am in the Father, and the Father is in me? The words I speak to you I do not speak on my own. The Father who dwells in me is working and speaking through me. Believe me when I tell you that I am in the Father and the Father is in me, or believe because of the works themselves. In truth, I tell you, whoever believes in me will do the works I do, and will do even greater ones than these, because I go to the Father. And whatever you ask in my name I will do for you, so that the Father's presence may be manifest in the Son. If you ask anything of me in my name, I will do it.

"If you love me, you will keep my commandments. And I will ask the Father, and He will give you another Advocate to be with you always, the Spirit of truth, which the world cannot accept, because it neither sees Him nor knows Him, but you know Him, because He remains with you and will be in you. I will not leave you orphans; I will come to you. In a little while the world will no longer see me, but you will see me, because I live and you will live. On that day you will realize that I am in my Father and you are in me, and I in you. The one who has my commandments and observes them is the one who loves me. And whoever loves me will be loved by my Father, and I will love him and make known my identity to him."

Judas, not the Iscariot, said to him, "Lord, what do you mean, you will reveal your identity to us and not to the world?"

Jesus explained to him. "Whoever loves me will keep my words, and my Father will love him, and we will come to him, and make our dwelling with him. Whoever does not love me does not keep my words. Yet the word that you hear is not my words, but the words of the Father who sent me.

"I have told you this while I am with you. The Advocate, the Holy Spirit, whom the Father will send in my name—He will teach you everything, and remind you of all that I have told you. Peace I leave with you; my peace I give you. Not as the world gives do I give to you. Do not let your hearts be troubled or afraid. You heard me tell you, 'I am going away and I will come back to you.' If you loved me you would rejoice that I am going to the Father, for the Father is greater than I. Now, I have told you these things before they happen, so that when they happen you may believe. I will speak no further with you, for the prince of this world approaches. But I assure you, he has no power over me, but the world must know that I love the Father and that what I am about to do is just as the Father had instructed me. So let us go, the time has come."

Jesus continued talking to them as they left. "I am the true vine; my Father is the vinedresser," he said to them. "Every branch in me that bears no fruit he strips away. Those branches that do bear fruit, he prunes so that they will bear even more fruit. You are already pruned because of the word that I have spoken to you. Remain in me as I remain in you. Just as the branch cannot bear fruit on its own, unless it remains in the vine, so neither can you bear fruit unless you remain in me. I am the vine and you are the branches. And since without me you can do nothing, whoever remains in me and I in him will bear much fruit. Anyone who does not remain in me will be like a withered branch that is good only for firewood. If you remain in me and my words remain in you, ask for whatever you want and it will be done for you. By this will my Father be glorified that as my disciples you bear much fruit. As the Father loves me, so I also love you. Remain in my love. If you keep my command to love, you will remain in my love, just as I have kept my Father's command, and remain in His love.

"I have told you this so that my joy might be in you and your joy might be complete. This is my commandment; that you love one another as I have loved you. No one has greater love than to lay down one's life for one's friends. You are my friends if you do what I command you. I have never called you slaves, because slaves do not know what is on their master's mind. I have called you friends, because I have told you everything I have heard from my Father. It was not you who chose me, but I who chose you, and appointed you to go and bear fruit that will last, so that whatever you ask the Father in my name He will give you. This is my command, that you love one another.

"If the world hates you, know that it hated me first. If you belonged to the world, the world would love its own. But, because you do not belong to the world, and I have chosen you out of the world, the world hates you. No slave is greater than his master, so if they persecuted me, they will persecute you also. If they kept my word they will keep yours as well. And they will do all these things to you because of me, because they do not know the One who sent me. If I had not come and spoken to them, they would be guilty of no sin. But now they have no excuse for their sin. Whoever hates me also hates my Father. If I had not done works among them that no other person ever did, they would have no sin. But, now they have seen and hated both my Father and me. But, this is happening that the word written in their law about me might be fulfilled, 'They hated me without cause.'

"I have told you this so that you may not lose heart. They will expel you from synagogues, and in fact, the time is coming when those who kill you will think they are offering worship to God. They will do this because they have not known either the Father or me. I tell you this so that when their time comes you will remember that I told you. I did not tell you these things earlier because I was with you, and it was not the time. But now I am leaving and going back to the One who sent me. I know that your hearts are heavy because I have told you these things, but it is important that I go. For, if I do not go, the Advocate will not come to you. If I go, I will send Him to you. And when He comes, He will indict the world of its sin, reveal God's righteousness manifest in me, and bring to an end the ruler of this world.

"I have much more to tell you, but you cannot bear it now. When He comes, however, the Spirit of truth, He will guide you to all that is true. He will not speak on His own, but will speak what He hears, and will declare to you the things that are to happen. He will bear witness to me, because He will take from me what is mine, and share it with you. Everything that the Father has is mine. That is why I tell you that He will take from me what is mine and share it with you.

"In a little while you will no longer see me. And again, in a little while you will see me." Some of his disciples said among themselves, "What is this 'little while' he is talking about? 'In a little while you will no longer see me, and again in a little while you will see me,' and 'I am going to the Father'? What is this 'little while'? We do not know what he means."

Jesus knew they were confused, so he said to them, "Are

you discussing among yourselves what I just said, 'In a little while you will not see me, and again in a little while you will see me'? In truth, I tell you, you will weep and mourn, while the world rejoices. You will grieve, but your grief will turn to joy. When a woman is in labor, she is in distress, because her hour has come. But once she has given birth to a child, she no longer remembers the pain because of her joy that a child has been born into the world. So you also are now in distress. But I will see you again, and your hearts will rejoice, and that joy no one will take from you. When that day comes, you will not have to question me about anything, for then you will know. But, for now, I tell you truthfully, whatever you ask in my name, my Father will give you. Until now you have not asked for anything in my name. Ask and you will receive, that your joy may be full.

"I have been telling you my thoughts in story form, but the time has come for me to speak to you, no longer in metaphors, but clearly about the Father. He is closer to you than you realize. When you talk to Him, He will listen to you, and grant you what you ask. You no longer have to ask in my name, for my Father knows you love me, and believe that I have come from Him. For this He loves you, and will grant you what you ask for.

"I came from the Father and have come into the world. Now I am leaving the world and will go back to my Father."

"Now that you are speaking clearly, and not in parables, we can understand you. We now realize that you know everything, and that there is no need for any of us to question you. We believe that you came from God."

Jesus picked them up on that, and asked, "Do you really believe? I tell you, the time is coming, and indeed is already here, when you will all be sent running each to his own home, and you will leave me alone, for it is written, 'I will strike the shepherd, and the sheep of his flock will be scattered.' But I am not alone, since the Father is always with me. I have told you this so that you might find peace in my intimacy with you. In the world you will have trouble, but there is no reason for you to be afraid, for I have already conquered the world. And, indeed, after I have been raised up, I shall go before you into Galilee."

Peter, then, said to him, "Though all may have their faith in you shaken, mine will never be." Jesus said to him, "The truth is, Peter, this very night, before the cock crows, you will deny me three times."

"Even though I should have to die with you, I will never deny you." And all the others said the same thing.

SIXTEEN

When Jesus had said this, he raised his eyes to heaven and said, "Father, the hour has finally come. Now is the time for you to recognize me before all, so that your son may show honor to you before all. Just as you gave him authority over all people, that he may give eternal life to all those you entrusted to him. Now, this is eternal life, that they should know you, the only true God, and the one whom you sent, Jesus, your anointed. I showed honor to you on earth by accomplishing the work you sent me to do. Now give glory to me with the eminence I had with you before the world began.

"I revealed your name to those you gave me out of the

world. They belonged to you and you gave them to me, and they have kept your word. Now they know that everything you gave me is from you, because the words you gave me I have given to them, and they accepted them and sincerely understood that I have come from you, and they believed that you have sent me. I now pray for them. I do not pray for the world, but for the ones you gave me, because they are yours. Of course everything of mine is yours, just as everything of yours is mine. In these friends of mine my presence and power will be proclaimed. And now I will no longer be in the world, but they are in the world, while I come to you. Holy Father, keep them in your name that you have given me, so that they may be one just as we are one. When I was with them I protected them in your name that you gave me, and I guarded them, and not one of them was lost, except the one who chose to be lost, that the scripture might be fulfilled. But now I am coming to you. I speak in the world that they may share my joy completely. I gave them your word, and the world has hated them already, because they do not belong to the world any more than I belong to the world. I do not ask that you take them out of the world, but that you keep them from evil. Consecrate them in the truth, and as your word is truth, consecrate them in your word. As you sent me into the world, so I sent them into the world, and I consecrate myself for them, that they also may be consecrated in truth.

"I pray not only for them, but also for those who will

believe in me through their word, so that they may all be one, as you, Father, are in me and I am in you, that they may also be in us, that the world may believe that you have sent me. And I gave them the recognition that you gave me, that they may be one as we are one; I in them, and you in me, that they may be brought to perfection as one, that the world may know that you sent me, and that you loved them even as you loved me. Father, they are your gift to me, and I wish that where I am they also may be there with me, that they may see the glory you have given me, because of the love you showed me even before the world began. Father of Goodness, the world does not know you, but I know you, and they know that you sent me. I made known to them your name and I will continue to make it known, that your love for me may be in them, and that I may be in them."

When Jesus said this, he went out with his disciples across the Kedron Valley to a place called Gethsemane, where there was a garden. "Sit down here while I go off and pray." He took with him Peter, and James and John, the sons of Zebedee, and began to feel sorrow and anguish. He then said to them, "My heart is filled with such sadness, I feel like dying. Stay near and watch with me." He went off a little farther and fell down on the ground and prayed, "Father, if it is possible, let this cup pass from me; yet not my will but as you will." When he went back to his disciples, he found them asleep. He said to them, "Could you not watch one hour with me? Watch and pray that you may not fall into temptation. The spirit is indeed willing, but the flesh is so weak." Going back to pray a second time, he said, "My Father, if it is not possible that this cup pass me by without my drinking it, then may your will be done."

He returned to the disciples a second time, and found them still asleep, for they looked weary-eyed. He left and went back to pray a third time, repeating what he had prayed before. Then he returned to his disciples and said to them, "Still sleeping, taking your rest? The time has come for the Son of Man to be betrayed to sinners. Get up, let us go. See, already my betrayer is here." Judas, his betrayer, knowing the place because Jesus had often met there with his disciples, came leading a band of soldiers and guards from the chief priests and the Pharisees. They approached with lanterns, torches, and weapons. Jesus, knowing everything that was going to happen to him, went out and said to them, "Who are you looking for?" "Jesus, the Nazorean." "Yahweh" (I AM he). Now Judas the traitor was with them. When Jesus said, "Yahweh" (I AM he), they were stunned and fell tripping over each other. So he said to them again, "Who are you looking for?" "Jesus the Nazorean." "I already told you that Yahweh [I AM he], so if it is me you want, let these men go." This was to fulfill what he had said, "No one of those whom you have given me have I lost."

Judas had arranged with them a sign. "The man I kiss is the one; seize him, and bind him immediately." Judas approached Jesus, saying to him, "Hail, Rabbi," and kissed him. Jesus responded, "Judas, you betray the Son of Man with a kiss? Get on with what you have come to do." Then the band of soldiers, the tribune, and the Judean guard quickly apprehended him and bound him. At that point Simon Peter, who had a sword, drew it, struck the high priest's servant, cutting off his right ear. The servant's name was Malchus. Jesus said to Peter, "Put up your sword into its sheath. Whoever lives by the sword will perish by the sword. Shall I not drink of the cup my Father has given me? Do you not think that if I asked my Father He would not provide me at this very moment with twelve legions of angels? But, then, how would the scriptures be fulfilled which say that it must happen this way." Bending down, Jesus reached out and touching the servant of the high priest, healed him.

Then Jesus said to the mob that had come to arrest him, "Have you come out as against a robber with swords and clubs to seize me? Daily I sat teaching in the temple precincts, yet no one laid a hand on me. I tell you, all that is happening now is so the writings of the prophets might be fulfilled." The disciples all left and fled. There was a young man there, wearing only a linen cloth about his body, who had followed Jesus. They seized him, but he left the cloth behind and ran off naked.

Then they led Jesus to Annas, the father-in-law of Caiaphas, who was the high priest that year. It was Caiaphas who had instructed the Judeans that it was better that one person should die rather than the whole nation suffer. There also came together the chief priests, the scribes, and the elders. Peter followed Jesus at a distance right into the courtyard of the high priest, and seated himself with the guards, warming himself by the fire. The chief priests and the entire Sanhedrin kept trying to obtain testimony against Jesus so they could put him to death, but they found none. Many came forward and gave false testimony against him, but their testimony did not agree. Some took the stand and testified falsely against him, saying, "We heard him say, 'I will destroy this temple built by human labor and in three days will rebuild it with no human effort.' " Even so, their testimony did not agree. The high priest rose before the assembly and questioned Jesus, saying, "Have you no answer? What are these men testifying against you?" But he remained silent and said nothing. Again the high priest asked him, "Are you the Messiah, the son of the Blessed One?" And he answered, "I am. And you will see the Son of Man seated at the right hand of the Power and coming with the clouds of heaven."

At that the chief priest tore open his garments and said, "What further need have we of witnesses? You yourselves have heard the blasphemy. What do you think?" And they all condemned him as deserving of death. Some began to spit on him. They blindfolded him and struck him, and said to him, "Prophesy!" And the guards struck him.

While Peter was below in the courtyard, one of the high priest's maids was passing by and saw Peter warming himself by the fire. She stared at him and said, "You were with him, the Nazorean, Jesus." But he denied it, saying, "I do not know what you are talking about." He then went out into the outer court. At that point the cock crowed. The maid noticed him, and said to the bystanders, "This man is one of them." Once again he denied it. A little later one of the slaves of the high priest, a relative of the man whose ear Peter slashed with the sword, said to Peter, "Surely you are one of them. Were you not in the garden with him? Your Galilean speech betrays you." Then he began to curse and to swear, "You do not know what you are talking about. I do not even know the man." And immediately a cock crowed a second time. Then Peter remembered the words that Jesus had said to him, "Before the cock crows twice you will deny me three times." Peter then went outside and wept bitterly.

SEVENTEEN

When morning came, all the chief priests and scribes as well as the elders of the people met and took counsel against Jesus to put him to death. They brought him before the Sanhedrin. They said, "If you are the Messiah, tell us." But he replied to them, "If I tell you, you will not believe, and if I question you, you will not respond, but I tell you, one day you will see the Son of Man seated at the right hand of the power of God." "Are you, then, the Son of God?" He replied to them, "You yourselves say that I am." Then they said, "What further need have we of witnesses, we have heard it from his own lips." Then they bound him, and led him away to Pilate, the governor.

Judas, who betrayed him, in the meantime, on learning that Jesus had been condemned, deeply regretted what he had done. He returned the thirty pieces of silver to the chief priests and elders, saying, "I have sinned in betraying innocent blood." They scoffed, "What is that to us? That is your problem." Flinging the money into the temple, he left and went off and hanged himself.

The chief priests picked up the money, but said, "It is not lawful to deposit it in the temple treasury, since it is the price of blood." After consulting over the matter, they used it to buy the potter's field as a burial place for strangers. That field to this day is called the Field of Blood. This all happened in fulfillment of the prophecy of Jeremiah: "And they took the thirty pieces of silver, the value of one with a price set on him, that children of Israel determined, and they bought with it the potter's field, just as the Lord had commanded me."

When they had brought Jesus from Caiaphas to the praetorium, they merely dropped him off, as they did not want to contaminate themselves so they could still eat the Passover meal. When Pilate, the governor, came out to them, he asked them, "What charge do you bring against this man?" They answered, "If he were not a criminal, we would not have brought him to you." Pilate said to them, "Take him and judge him according to your law."

They answered him, "We do not have the right to execute anyone," this fulfilling Jesus' words indicating the kind of death he would die. Then they brought charges against him, saying, "We found this man subverting the people. He opposes paying taxes to Caesar, and maintains that he is the Messiah, a king." So Pilate went back into the praetorium and summoned Jesus. "Are you the King of the Judeans?" Jesus answered, "Do you say this on your own, or have others told you about me?"

"Am I a Judean? Your own people and your chief priests have turned you over to me. What have you done?"

Jesus answered, "My kingdom is not of this world. If I were, my attendants would be only too glad to fight and keep me from being turned out to the Judeans. But my kingdom is not from here."

Then Pilate said, "Then, you are a king?"

Jesus answered, "You say I am a king. For this I was born, and for this I have come into the world, so that I might testify to the truth. Everyone who belongs to the truth listens to my voice." Pilate said to him, "What is truth?"

When he had said this, he went out to the Judeans and said to them, "I find no guilt in him." And Jesus replied, "It is you who say it." And when the chief priests and elders accused him, he said nothing. Then Pilate said to him, "Do you not hear all the charges that they are bringing against you?" But he still said nothing, not even one word, which astonished the governor.

Pilate then addressed the chief priests and the crowd. "I

find no guilt in this man." But they were adamant. "He is inciting the people with his teaching all throughout Judea, from Galilee, where he began, even down to this very place." On hearing this, Pilate asked if the man was a Galilean. Upon learning that he was under Herod's jurisdiction, he sent him to Herod, who was in Jerusalem at the time. Herod was excited to see Jesus, as he had wanted to see Jesus for a long time. He had heard about him and was hoping to see him perform some miracle. Herod questioned Jesus at length, but Jesus gave him no answer. The chief priests and scribes, meanwhile, stood there, accusing Jesus vehemently.

On the occasion of the festival, it was the custom of the governor to release to the crowd one prisoner whomsoever they wished. At the time they had a notorious prisoner named Barabbas. So when they had all assembled, Pilate asked them, "Which one do you want me to release to you, Barabbas, or Jesus called Messiah?" For he knew it was out of envy that they had delivered him up. In the meantime, while Pilate was still holding court, his wife sent him a message: "Have nothing to do with that righteous man, as I have suffered terribly in a dream today because of him."

The chief priests and the elders had persuaded the crowds to ask for Barabbas but to destroy Jesus. So when the governor asked the crowd "Which of the two do you wish me to release?" they answered, "Barabbas." Pilate then said to them, "Then what shall I do with Jesus, called Messiah?" "Crucify him!" "Why, what evil has he done?" And they shouted all the louder, "Crucify him!" When Pilate realized he was accomplishing nothing, but that the crowd was on the verge of rioting, he took water and washed his hands in front of the whole crowd, saying, "I am innocent of this man's blood. It is now your problem." Then the whole people replied, "His blood be upon us and upon our children." Finally, he released Barabbas to them. Then Pilate took Jesus and ordered him to be flogged. The soldiers wove a crown made of thorny branches and placed it on his head, and clothed him in a purple cloak, then, parading up to him, they saluted him, "Hail, king of the Judeans!" And they took turns beating him with a lash.

Once more Pilate went out and said to them, "Look, I am bringing him out to you to show you I find no guilt in him." So Jesus came out wearing the purple cloak, with the crown of thorns on his head, and he said to them, "Behold the man!" When the chief priests and the guards saw him, they cried out, "Crucify him! Crucify him!"

Pilate then said to them, "Take him yourself and crucify him. I find no guilt in him." The Judeans answered, "We have a law, and according to that law he must be put to death, because he has made himself out to be the Son of God." Now, when Pilate heard that remark, he became even more afraid, and went back into the praetorium and asked Jesus, "Where are you from?" Jesus did not answer him. Then Pilate said, "Do you not know that I have the power to release you or to crucify you?"

Jesus answered him, "You would have no power over me were it not given to you from above, and for this reason those who handed me over to you have the greater sin." After that, Pilate tried again to release him, but the Judeans shouted out, "If you release him, you are no friend of Caesar's. Everyone who declares himself a king opposes Caesar."

Hearing this, Pilate then had Jesus brought out and took his seat at the judge's bench on the Stone Floor, in Hebrew called *Gabbatha*. It was preparation day for Passover, and it was about noon. He said to the Judeans, "Behold, your king!" They cried out, "Take him away, take him away! Crucify him!"

Pilate said to them, "Shall I crucify your king?" The chief priests answered, "We have no king but Caesar." Then he handed him over to them to be crucified.

So they took Jesus, and carrying the cross himself, he went out to what is called the Place of the Skull, in Hebrew, Golgotha. On the way, they came across a certain man by the name of Simon, a Cyrenian, who was coming in from the country. They forced him to assist in carrying the cross behind Jesus. There was also a large crowd following Jesus, among them many women who mourned and lamented him. Jesus turned to them and said, "Daughters of Jerusalem, do not weep for me; weep for yourselves and for your children. For, I tell you, the days are coming when people will say, 'Fortunate are the barren, the wombs that never bore and the breasts that never nursed.' At that time people will say to the mountains, 'Fall on us!' and to the hills, 'Cover us!' for if these things are done when the wood is green, what will happen when it is dry."

Now there were two others, both criminals, who were led away with Jesus to be executed. When they arrived at Golgotha, they crucified him and the criminals, one on his right and one on his left. Pilate also had an inscription written and put on the cross. It read, "Jesus, the Nazorean, King of the Judeans." Many of the Judeans read the inscription because the place where Jesus was crucified was near the city, and it was written in Hebrew, Greek, and Latin. So the chief priests protested to Pilate, "Do not write 'The King of the Judeans,' but 'he said, I am the King of the Judeans.' " Pilate answered, "What I have written, I have written."

When the soldiers crucified Jesus, he said, "Father, forgive them, for they know not what they do." They then took his clothes and divided them among themselves four ways. They then took his tunic, but since it was without a seam, and woven in one piece from top to bottom, they said to one another, "Let's not tear it, but cast lots for it to see whose it will be," which they then did, thus fulfilling the scripture passage, "They divided my garments among them and for my vesture they cast lots."

The people stood by and watched. The rulers jeered at him. "He saved others, let him save himself if he is the chosen one, the Anointed of God." Even the soldiers ridiculed him. As they came close to offer him wine, they called out, "If you are the King of the Judeans, save yourself." Above him was the inscription that read "This is the King of the Judeans."

Standing by the cross of Jesus were his mother and his mother's sister, Mary, the wife of Clopas, and Mary from Magdala. When Jesus saw his mother and the disciple there whom he loved, he said to his mother, "Woman, behold, your son." Then he said to the disciple, "Son, behold, your mother." From that moment the disciple took her into his care.

One of the criminals hanging there made fun of Jesus, saying, "Are you not the Messiah? Save yourself, then, and us as well." The other, however, rebuked him. "Have you no fear of God, for you are under the same sentence? We, alas, have been condemned justly, for crimes we committed, but this man has done nothing." Then he said to Jesus, "Jesus, remember me when you come into your kingdom." He replied, "In truth, I say to you, this very day you will be with me in paradise."

After this, aware that everything was now finished, in order that the scripture might be fulfilled, Jesus said, "I thirst." There was a vessel filled with common wine, so they put a sponge soaked in the wine on a stick of hyssop and put it up to his mouth. When Jesus had taken the wine, he said, "It is finished."

It was now about noon, and darkness covered the whole earth until three in the afternoon, because of an eclipse of the sun. Then the veil of the temple was torn in two. Jesus cried out in a loud voice, "Father, into your hands I commend my spirit"; and when he had said that, he breathed forth his spirit. The centurion who witnessed what had taken place bore witness to God, and said, "This man was beyond doubt innocent." When all the people standing by saw all that had happened, they went home beating their breasts. All Jesus' acquaintances, including the women who had followed him from Galilee, stood at a distance, witnessing all that was taking place.

Since it was preparation day, in order that the bodies might not remain on the cross on the sabbath, for the sabbath of that week was a solemn one, the Judeans asked Pilate that their legs be broken and they be taken down. So, the soldiers came and broke the legs of the first, and then of the other one who was crucified with Jesus. But when they came to Jesus and saw that he was already dead, they did not break his legs, but one of the soldiers thrust his spear into his side and immediately blood and water flowed out. An eyewitness has testified, and his testimony is true. He knows that he speaks the truth, so that you also may come to believe. For this happened so that the scripture passage might be fulfilled, "Not a bone of his will be broken," and again another scripture passage says, "They will look on him whom they have pierced."

Now, there was a wealthy and holy man named Joseph, who, though a member of the Sanhedrin, had not consented to their plot to kill Jesus. He came from the Jewish town of Arimathea and was awaiting the coming of the kingdom of God. He boldly went to Pilate and asked for the body of Jesus. Pilate was surprised that he was already dead. He summoned the centurion and asked if Jesus had already died, and when he had assured him he had, he gave the body to Joseph. Nicodemus, the one who had come to Jesus late at night, also came bringing a mixture of myrrh and aloes, about a hundred pounds. Joseph brought a linen cloth, which he had just purchased. They took the body down from the cross and wrapped it in the linen cloth and the spices, according to Judean burial custom, and laid it in the new tomb, which Joseph had hewn out of the rock, in which no one had yet been buried. The tomb was located in a garden. They then rolled a stone against the entrance to the tomb, and left. Mary from Magdala and Mary, the mother of Joses, who had come from Galilee with Jesus, watched where he was laid, and how the body was placed in the tomb. They left and prepared spices and oil so they could later on anoint the body. It was the day of preparation, and the sabbath was about to begin, so they rested on the sabbath as instructed by the commandment.

EIGHTEEN

At daybreak on the first day of the week, Mary from Magdala, and Mary, the mother of James, and Salome took the spices they had prepared and went to the tomb. They were saying to one another, "Who will roll back the stone for us from the entrance to the tomb?" However, they found the stone rolled away from the tomb; but when they entered, they did not find the body of the Lord Jesus. While they were wondering about this, to their surprise, two men in dazzling garments appeared to them. The women were terrified, and bowed their faces to the ground. They said to them, "Why do you seek the living among the dead? He is not here; he has been raised. Remember what he said to you when he was still in Galilee, that the Son of Man must be handed over to sinners and be crucified, and rise on the third day." And they remembered his words.

They then returned from the tomb and told what had happened to the eleven and to all the others. The women were Mary from Magdala, Joanna, and Mary, the mother of James. The others who accompanied them also told this to the apostles, but their story seemed like nonsense and they did not believe them.

Peter, however, and the other disciple, the one whom Jesus loved, got up and ran to the tomb. The other disciple reached the tomb first, bent down, and saw the burial clothes there but did not go in. When Simon Peter arrived, he went into the tomb and saw the burial clothes there, and the cloth that had covered the head, not with the burial clothes, but rolled up in a separate place. Then the other disciple also went in, the one who arrived at the tomb first, and he saw and believed. For they had not yet understood the scripture that he had to rise from the dead. Then the disciples returned home.

Mary, however, stayed outside the tomb, weeping. As she wept, she bent over into the tomb and saw two angels in white sitting there, one at the head and one at the feet, where the body of Jesus had been. And they said to her, "Woman, why are you weeping?" She said, "They have taken my Lord, and I don't know where they have laid him." When she had said this, she turned around and saw Jesus there but did not know it was Jesus. He said to her, "Woman, why are you weeping? For whom are you looking?" Thinking it was the gardener, she said, "Sir, if you carried him away, tell me where you have laid him and I will take him." Then Jesus said to her, "Mary." She turned and said to him in Hebrew, *"Rabbouni!* My dear Master!" Jesus said to her, "Do not cling to me, for I have not yet ascended to the Father. Now go and tell my brothers 'I am going to my Father and your Father, to my God and your God.'" Mary left and told the disciples, "I have seen the Lord," and also what he had said to her.

Later that day, two of the disciples were going to Emmaus, a village seven miles from Jerusalem. As they went along, they were talking about all the things that had taken place. While they were talking and arguing, Jesus himself drew near and walked with them, but they did not recognize him. He asked them, "What are you discussing as you walk along?" Being depressed, and surprised at the question, they stopped, and one of them, Clopas by name, said to him, "Are you the only visitor to Jerusalem who does not know of the things that have been taking place there the past few days?"

"What kind of things?" he asked. And they said to him, "About Jesus from Nazareth, who was a prophet powerful in words and miracles, in God's eyes as well as in the eyes of all the people, and how our chief priests and rulers had him condemned to death and crucified. We had been hoping he was the one who would redeem Israel. Besides all this, it is now the third day since this took place. Some of our woman companions shocked us by telling us they had been at the tomb early this morning but did not find his body. They came back and reported that they had seen a vision of angels, who told them that he was alive. Then some of those among us went to the tomb and indeed found it just as the women had said, but him we did not see."

Then he said to them, "Oh, how foolish you are! How slow of heart to believe all that the prophets have said! Was it not necessary that the Messiah should suffer these things before entering into his glory?" Then, beginning with Moses down through all the prophets, he interpreted for them all that was written about him in the scriptures. As they approached the village to which they were going, he gave the impression he was continuing on his way, so they urged him, "Stay with us, for it is nearly nightfall and the day is almost over." So he went in to stay with them. While he was at table with them, he took bread, blessed it, broke it, and gave it to them. With that their eyes were opened and they recognized him. He then vanished from their sight. Then they said to each other, "Were not our hearts burning within us while he spoke to us along the way, and opened for us the scriptures?"

They set out at once for Jerusalem, where they found the Eleven and those gathered with them, who began telling them, "The Lord has been truly raised and has appeared to

Simon!" Then the two recounted what had taken place on the way, and how he was made known to them in the breaking of the bread.

While they were still speaking about this, he stood in their midst and said to them, "Peace be with you." But they were shocked and terrified, thinking they were seeing a ghost. Then he said to them, "Why are you upset, and why do you question deep down in your hearts? Look at my hands and feet and see that it is I myself. Touch me and see, because a ghost does not have flesh and bones as you can see I have."

As he said this, he showed them his hands and feet. Still they found it hard to believe; though thrilled that it might possibly be he, he asked them, "Have you anything here to eat?" They gave him a piece of roasted fish, which he took and ate in front of them. He then spoke to them. "These are my words that I spoke to you while I was still with you, that everything written about me in the law of Moses and in the prophets and psalms had to be fulfilled." Then he opened their minds to understand the scriptures. And he said to them, "Thus it is written that the Messiah would suffer and rise from the dead on the third day, and that repentance for the forgiveness of sins would be preached in his name to all the nations, beginning from Jerusalem. You are witnesses to these happenings. As the Father has sent me, so I now send you." Then, breathing upon them, he said to them, "Receive the Holy Spirit. Whose sins you shall forgive they are forgiven them, and whose sins you shall retain, they are retained." He then said to them, "Go into the whole world and proclaim the good news to every creature. Whoever believes and is baptized will be saved; whoever does not believe will be condemned. These signs will accompany those who believe: In my name they will drive out devils, they will speak new languages. They will pick up serpents, and if they drink any deadly thing, it will not harm them. They will lay hands on the sick, and they will recover. And I send the promise of my Father upon you. However, stay here in the city until you are clothed with power from on high."

Thomas, called Didymus, the twin, one of the Twelve, was not with them when Jesus came. So, the other disciples told him, "We have seen the Lord." But he said to them, "Unless I see the mark of the nails in his hands and put my finger into the nailmarks in his hands, and my hand into his side, I will not believe."

A week later, his disciples were again inside and Thomas was with them. Jesus came, although the doors were locked, and stood in their midst and said, "Peace be with you." Then he said to Thomas, "Thomas, put your finger here and see my hands, and bring your hand and put it into my side, and be not unbelieving, but believe."

Thomas answered and said to him, "My Lord and my God!"

Jesus said to him, "Thomas, you believe because you have seen. Blessed are those who believe but have not seen."

Now, Jesus did many other things in the presence of his disciples that are not written in this book. But these have been written, so that you may come to believe that Jesus is the Messiah, the Son of God, and that through this belief you may have life in his name.

After this Jesus appeared again to his disciples at the sea of Tiberias (Galilee). He manifested himself in this way. Simon Peter, Thomas called Didymus, Nathaniel from Cana in Galilee, Zebedee's sons (James and John), and two other disciples, were together. Simon Peter said, "I am going fishing." The others said, "We will go with you." So they went and climbed into the boat, but after fishing all night, they caught nothing. When dawn came, they had still caught nothing. Jesus was standing on the shore, although they did not realize it was Jesus. He called out to them, "Young men, have you caught anything to eat?" "Not a thing," they called back.

"Cast your net over the right side of the boat and you will find something." So they cast their net and were not able to pull it in because of the number of fish. So the disciple whom Jesus loved said to Peter, "It is the Lord." When Simon Peter heard that it was the Lord, he threw on his robe, for he was naked, and jumped into the water. The other disciples brought in the boat, for they were not far

from shore, only about a hundred yards. They were drag-
ging the net full of fish alongside the boat.

When they climbed out onto the shore, they saw a char-
coal fire with fish on it and bread. Jesus said to them, "Bring
some of the fish you just caught." Then Simon Peter went
over and dragged the net ashore full with a hundred fifty-
three large fish. Even though there were so many, the net
did not break.

Jesus said to them, "Come, let us eat our breakfast."
None of the disciples dared to ask him, "Who are you?" for
they realized it was the Lord. Jesus came over and took the
bread and gave it to them, and the same with the fish. This
was now the third time Jesus appeared to his disciples after
being raised from the dead.

When they had finished breakfast, Jesus said to Simon
Peter, "Simon, son of John, do you love me more than
these?" "Yes, Lord, you know that I love you." "Feed my
lambs!" He then said to him a second time, "Simon, son of
John, do you love me?" "Yes, Lord, you know that I love
you." "Care for my sheep." Then he said to him a third
time, "Simon, son of John, do you love me?" Peter was
deeply hurt that Jesus should ask him a third time "Do you
love me?" and he said to him, "Lord, you know everything;
you know that I love you." Then Jesus said to him, "Feed
my sheep. In truth, I tell you, when you were younger you
used to tie your own belt, and go where you wished. But
when you grow old, you will stretch out your hands and

someone else will gird you and lead you where you do not wish to go." He said this signifying the kind of death by which he would give honor to God. After he said this, he told Peter, "Follow me."

Peter then turned and saw the other disciple following, the one Jesus loved, the one who had reclined on his shoulder during the supper, and had asked, "Master, who is the one who will betray you?" When Peter saw him, he said to Jesus, "Lord, what about him?" Jesus said to him, "What if I want him to remain until I come? What concern is that of yours? You just follow me." So the word spread among the brothers that that disciple would not die. But Jesus had not told him that he would not die, only "What if I want him to remain until I come? What concern is that of yours?"

It is this disciple who testifies to these things and has written them, and we know that his testimony is true. There are also many other things that Jesus did, but if these were to be described individually, I think the whole world could not contain all the books that would have to be written.

Then he led them out as far as Bethany, raised his hands, and blessed them. As he was blessing them, he parted from them and was taken up to heaven. They did him homage and then returned to Jerusalem filled with joy. And they were continually in the temple praising God.

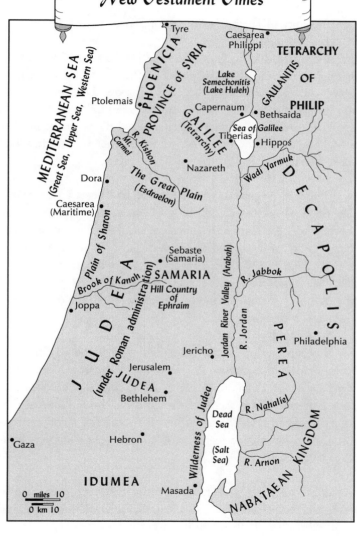

PALESTINE
New Testament Times

Tyre

Caesarea Philippi

TETRARCHY

OF

PHILIP

PHOENICIA

PROVINCE of SYRIA

GAULANITIS

Lake Semechonitis (Lake Huleh)

MEDITERRANEAN SEA
(Great Sea, Upper Sea, Western Sea)

Ptolemais

GALILEE (Tetrarchy)

Capernaum

Bethsaida

Sea of Galilee

Tiberias

Hippos

Mt. Carmel

R. Kishon

Nazareth

Wadi Yarmuk

Dora

The Great Plain (Esdraelon)

D E C A P O L I S

Caesarea (Maritime)

Plain of Sharon

Sebaste (Samaria)

SAMARIA

R. Jabbok

Brook of Kanah

Hill Country of Ephraim

Jordan River Valley (Arabah)

Joppa

J U D E A
(under Roman administration)

R. Jordan

P E R E A

Jericho

Philadelphia

Jerusalem

JUDEA

Bethlehem

Wilderness of Judea

Dead Sea

R. Nahaliel

Gaza

Hebron

(Salt Sea)

R. Arnon

IDUMEA

Masada

NABATAEAN KINGDOM

0 miles 10

0 km 10

The Ancestry of Jesus

The genealogy of Jesus Christ, son of David, son of Abraham:

Abraham fathered Isaac, Isaac fathered Jacob, Jacob fathered Judah and his brothers, Judah fathered Perez and Zerah, whose mother was Tamar, Perez fathered Hezron, Hezron fathered Ram, Ram fathered Amminadab, Amminadab fathered Nahshon, Nahshon fathered Salmon, Salmon fathered Boaz, whose mother was Rahab, Boaz fathered Obed, whose mother was Ruth, Obed fathered Jesse; and Jesse fathered King David.

David fathered Solomon, whose mother had been Uriah's wife, Solomon fathered Rehoboam, Rehoboam fathered Abijah, Abijah fathered Asa, Asa fathered Jehoshaphat, Jehoshaphat fathered Joram, Joram fathered Uzziah, Uzziah fathered Jotham, Jotham fathered Ahaz, Ahaz fathered Hezekiah, Hezekiah fathered Manasseh, Manasseh fathered Amon, Amon fathered Josiah; and Josiah fathered Jechoniah and his brothers. Then the deportation to Babylon took place.

After the deportation to Babylon: Jachoniah fathered Shealtiel, Shealtiel fathered Zerubbabel, Zerubbabel fathered Abiud, Abiud fathered Eliakim, Eliakim fathered Azor, Azor fathered Zadok, Zadok fathered Achim, Achim fathered Eliud, Eliud fathered Eleazar, Eleazar fathered Matthan, Matthan fathered Jacob; and Jacob fathered Joseph the husband of Mary; of her was born Jesus who is called Christ.

The sum of generations is therefore: fourteen from Abraham to David; fourteen from David to the Babylonian deportation; and fourteen from the Babylonian deportation to Christ.